Title Page

Real Estate Revolution

by

Patrick Palzkill

Copyright

Disclosure

The author is a real estate broker licensed in Massachusetts (MA License #9186). The author is not an attorney or a mortgage originator. Real estate laws, customs, and practices vary by state; readers are encouraged to consult qualified professionals in their own jurisdiction. Always consult an attorney for legal advice.

In the interest of full transparency and as required by law, the following disclosures apply to real estate brokerage commissions:

There is no standard, fixed, or required commission rate in real estate transactions. All commission rates and total compensation paid to real estate brokers are fully negotiable between the client and the broker.

While this book may reference a total listing and/or buyer broker commission range of approximately 5–6%* of the final net sales price, this range is provided for general informational purposes only and is not a guarantee. Actual commission rates and total compensation may be higher, lower, or structured differently, and may vary based on factors including, but not limited to:

- Market conditions at the time of the transaction.
- Concessions or incentives offered to facilitate a sale.
- The complexity or unique circumstances of the transaction.
- The terms of any written agreement between the client and their brokerage firm or any cooperating broker.

Any offer of compensation to a buyer's broker or cooperating broker is made solely at the direction of the seller and is fully negotiable. Sellers are not required to offer any specific amount or percentage of compensation and may choose to offer little or no compensation to a cooperating broker.

All examples, illustrations, and projections contained in this book are for informational purposes only and are not guarantees.

All documents referenced are sample materials provided for educational purposes only and are not intended to be used as legal documents.

Visit https://www.realestaterevolution.org/ for more information.

Dedication

Your Real Estate Reference Guide

Dedicated to my family. My Tribe, my friends of lifelong learning.

Patrick Palzkill

Dreamer, child, brother, Christian, dog lover, dishwasher, farmer, chicken feeder, gardener, landscaper, painter, tractor driver, cowboy, equestrian, bull rider, fence builder, carpenter, truck driver, mechanic, fisherman, hunter, runner, veterinarian, pallbearer, student, teacher, soccer player, state champion wrestling team, Olympic hopeful, state champion parliamentarian, speaker, songwriter, bartender, Optimist, cement mason, banker, loan officer, real estate agent, broker, homeowner, landlord, MBA graduate, traveler, Promise Keeper, husband, father, coach, volunteer, technical biographer, historian, insurance broker, stock broker, financial advisor, registered principal, lighting designer, marketing consultant, Las Vegas variety show producer, beachcomber, author.

50 years of stories and thousands of deals – this book can help you navigate forward toward owning your own piece of America.

We need borders, fences, and lot lines because of "wants" vs. "needs." It's just the way it is. We discuss that in Chapter 10.

It's been this way since time began. Once someone commits to a community, signs their name, and starts to improve a territory, a land, a home – we naturally protect that territory. Boundaries show physical territory and designate the set of rules the tribe imposes over that territory to facilitate their needs.

Needs include:

Clean Air

Clean Water

Clean Food

Clean Thermoregulated Shelter

Clothing and Electricity

Safety and Human Belonging

The ability to maintain a Healthy Body, Love, Intimacy and Social Connection

Working together — We can do this.

Introduction

This book is a manifesto that finally drags the real estate industry into the sunlight and hands the power back to the American home buyer and seller. Think Rich Dad Poor Dad meets The Big Short – but for housing. Provocative, unapologetic, financially empowering, and written with the fire of someone who has spent 50+ years as a steward of the land, watching good people get abused by a system that was never designed to serve them.

Our mission is crystal clear: As a TRUE fiduciary to the consumer, expose the rigged game. Arm readers with weapons-grade knowledge and tactics. Show them exactly how to buy or sell a home on their terms, possibly keep tens of thousands of dollars in their own pockets, and reclaim the American Dream that has been gatekept by high commissions and outdated political tax structures for far too long.

We look at the new National Association of Realtors (NAR) rules that apply in 2026, as well as how AI and Robotics may affect where you live and how you live.

We look at the dramatic changes the thirst for a "homeland" has affected world history. We look at the acquisition of real estate in the Americas, from our past experiences gleaned from the Declaration of Independence, now on the 250th anniversary of the American Revolution. We also discuss ideas, strategies and actions we can take today and in the future to build Sustainable Cities, free of misunderstandings on who owns what and what rights these particular people have. We discuss why it's so important that we start today and do it for our children's future.

If you look at life on Earth today, it's not uncommon to see unsustainable toxic cities, where waste and debt have built up and destroyed the environment around them, and how quickly it happened. For example, the Chernobyl and Three Mile Island nuclear energy disasters. Paris, London and much of Europe will never be rebuilt into a sustainable city. In the US, millions of underground oil tanks from the 1970's and residue from lead paint and old water pipes in many homes built before 1978. Nagasaki, Vietnam, and Ukraine are just a few of the many wars that destroy cultures, and all are biological examples of unsustainable environments.

It happens quickly. Think of the algae bloom on a lake. It starts out small and then progresses with either arithmetic/linear or exponential/geometric progression. It's usually exponential in nature. One day the pond is ¼ covered, the next day it's entirely covered.

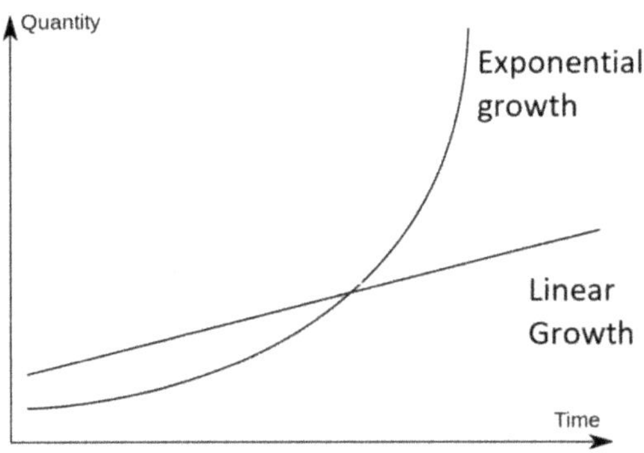

To understand linear/arithmetic, think of the annual growth rings in trees. They are roughly equal in width under stable conditions, adding a constant layer each year (radial distance from center increases linearly).

These represent additive, steady accumulation rather than explosive increase.

Geometric Progression (Exponential Growth) in Nature

Geometric progressions are far more common in biological growth, especially when resources are unlimited:

• Population growth: Bacterial colonies, insects, or animal populations in ideal conditions double (or multiply by a fixed ratio) each generation, leading to exponential increase.

• Cell division: In embryonic development or microbial repro- duction, cells divide mitotically—one becomes two, two become four, etc. (common ratio of 2).

• Spread of viruses or epidemics: Each infected individual spreads to a fixed average number of others.

In reality, exponential growth eventually slows due to resource limits, forming an S-shaped (logistic) curve, but the initial phase is geometric.

Many of our big cities in the US (and around the world) are in advanced decay — i.e. reaching resource limits. They have ballooning budget deficits, schools on all levels that don't function, unfunded pensions, and crime that inhibits the ability to live by our God given rights of life, liberty and the pursuit of happiness. (see chapter 11)

Life — as in having the ability to enjoy time with your family and friends and not be a slave to your job.

Liberty — as in being free to roam without fear from undue influences.

Pursuit of happiness without excessive financial burden or governmental intervention.

Clearly communicate with others in an open manner or in a private manner, as so disclosed. And finally, access to a peaceful society that has the thirst for lifelong learning.

That's what's in the book. I hope you enjoy it and join the revolution. It starts today.

*The author is a real estate broker, licensed in Massachusetts and is not an attorney. The items listed below reflect common U.S. landlord-tenant frameworks and are subject to state and local law. Always verify jurisdiction-specific statutes before acting.

Here are the 25 most important rights that a tenant normally does NOT have** (i.e., rights that belong exclusively or primarily to the landlord/property owner, even in tenant-friendly states like Massachusetts, California, New York, etc.). These are the ones tenants most often misunderstand or try to claim they have — but legally do not, depending on the contract.

- A tenant cannot unilaterally reduce or withhold rent simply because they "don't like" something (they must pay and sue or use legal processes).
- Tenant cannot change the locks or deny the landlord all access.
- Tenant cannot refuse entry for repairs or inspections when proper notice is given.
- Tenant cannot sublet or Airbnb the unit without landlord's written permission.
- Tenant cannot add roommates or long-term guests not on the original lease without approval.
- Tenant cannot refuse to pay rent increases that are legally noticed.
- Tenant cannot stay past the end of a fixed-term lease without the landlord's approval to renew.
- Tenant cannot make structural alterations, knock down walls, or rewire electricity.
- Tenant cannot install permanent fixtures (built-ins, hardwired lighting, etc.) and claim them as theirs.
- Tenant cannot refuse to return keys or garage openers at move-out.
- Tenant cannot demand the landlord pay for tenant's personal property damage (furniture, electronics, etc.).
- Tenant cannot refuse to allow showings to new tenants or buyers with proper notice.
- Tenant cannot dictate what the landlord does with the property after the lease ends (sell, renovate, live in it, etc.).
- Tenant cannot prevent the landlord from selling or mortgaging the property.
- Tenant cannot stop a legal eviction once a judge has ruled.
- Tenant cannot refuse to vacate after losing an eviction case (sheriff will remove them).
- Tenant cannot unilaterally "break" a fixed-term lease without penalty (landlord can sue for remaining rent in most states).
- Tenant cannot demand the security deposit back before move-out inspection is complete.
- Tenant cannot paint, drill large holes, or renovate without written permission.
- Tenant cannot run a business out of a residential unit if the lease or zoning prohibits it.
- Tenant cannot install a pool, hot tub, or trampoline without permission.

• Tenant cannot refuse to pay for damage they or their guests caused.

• Tenant cannot demand the landlord upgrade appliances or finishes just because they're "old".

• Tenant cannot prevent the landlord from raising rent to market rate at lease renewal (in non-rent-controlled areas).

• Tenant has no ownership interest — they cannot claim the property via "adverse possession" simply by living there and paying rent.

• These 25 issues are the ones that cause 95% of landlord-tenant disputes. Tenants often believe (or are told on social media) they have these rights — but under U.S. law, they do not. The landlord retains ultimate control and ownership at all times; the tenant only has a temporary, revocable license to occupy under the owner's terms.

Here is a list of 100 fundamental rights that a landlord or property owner generally has over a tenant** (focused primarily on U.S. residential rental law, especially in landlord-friendly or neutral states like Massachusetts). These are the core advantages and powers the owner retains even after leasing the property to a tenant, depending on the contract.

• Right to receive rent on time and in full.

• Right to charge late fees if rent is not paid when due.

• Right to collect a security deposit (usually 1–2 months' rent).

• Right to deduct from the security deposit for unpaid rent or damage beyond normal wear and tear.

• Right to set the amount of rent (in non-rent-controlled areas).

• Right to increase rent with proper notice (typically 30–60 days or one full rental period).

• Right to refuse to renew a lease at the end of its term (in most states).

• Right to evict for non-payment of rent.

• Right to evict for lease violations.

• Right to evict for criminal or drug-related activity on the premises.

• Right to evict a holdover tenant after the lease expires.

• Right to enter the property with proper notice (usually 24 hours) for inspections, repairs, or showings.

• Right to enter without notice in emergencies (fire, flood, etc.).

• Right to approve or deny subletting or assignment of the lease.

• Right to approve or deny additional occupants or roommates not on the original lease.

• Right to require renter's insurance.

• Right to prohibit certain pets or charge pet fees/deposits.

• Right to set reasonable rules and regulations for the property.

• Right to enforce quiet enjoyment for other tenants/neighbors.

• Right to restrict commercial use of a residential unit.

• Right to prohibit illegal activity on the premises.

• Right to require the tenant to maintain the yard/grounds (if applicable).

• Right to demand the tenant maintain the interior in clean and sanitary condition.

• Right to prohibit alterations or painting without written permission.

• Right to prohibit installation of fixtures without permission.

• Right to require removal of tenant-installed fixtures at move-out.

• Right to collect application fees and run background/credit checks.

• Right to reject applicants based on credit, rental history, or income.

• Right to require all adult occupants to sign the lease or be approved.

• Right to terminate a month-to-month tenancy with proper notice (usually 30 days).

• Right to collect the full term rent in a fixed-term lease if tenant breaks the lease early (in most states).

• Right to re-key or change locks between tenancies.

• Right to place a lien on tenant's personal property for unpaid rent (in some states).

• Right to sell the property while it is tenant-occupied.

• Right to show the property to prospective buyers or new tenants with proper notice.

• Right to mortgage or refinance the property without tenant approval.

• Right to decide whether utilities are included or tenant-paid.

• Right to shut off utilities only under very limited legal circumstances (almost never allowed).

• Right to choose which repairs are tenant responsibility vs. landlord responsibility.

• Right to access the unit to make repairs the tenant refuses to allow.

• Right to deduct repair costs from the security deposit if tenant caused damage.

• Right to require professional carpet cleaning at move-out (if stated in lease).

• Right to charge cleaning fees if unit is left excessively dirty.

• Right to prohibit smoking inside the unit or on the premises.

• Right to prohibit waterbeds or other high-risk items.

• Right to set guest stay limits (e.g., no guests longer than 14 days).

• Right to restrict satellite dishes or external antennas (within FCC limits).

• Right to require tenant to carry liability insurance.

• Right to collect last month's rent upfront (in many states).

• Right to refuse emotional support animals that pose a direct threat or cause substantial damage (with documentation).

• Right to approve or deny reasonable accommodation/modification requests if they impose undue burden.

• Right to collect NSF/check bounce fees.

• Right to require payment by specific methods (no cash, etc.).

• Right to refuse personal guarantees after the initial lease signing.

• Right to refuse cosigners unless originally required.

• Right to take possession immediately after a court-ordered eviction.

• Right to dispose of abandoned property after following state law.

• Right to charge storage fees for property left behind.

• Right to sue tenant for unpaid rent or damages in court.

• Right to report unpaid rent or evictions to credit bureaus.

• Right to report tenant payment history (good or bad) to tenant screening services.

• Right to place "For Rent" or "For Sale" signs on the property.

• Right to install security cameras in common areas.

• Right to restrict parking to assigned spaces only.

• Right to tow illegally parked vehicles at tenant's expense.

• Right to prohibit Airbnb or short-term subletting.

• Right to prohibit hoarding or excessive personal property that creates hazards.

• Right to require tenant to shovel snow or mow lawn (if in lease).

• Right to restrict holiday decorations that cause damage.

• Right to prohibit nails/screws in walls or require spackle/paint at move-out.

• Right to require all keys and garage openers returned at move-out.

• Right to charge for lost keys or re-keying.

• Right to decide whether to allow grills on balconies or patios.

• Right to prohibit candles or open flames.

• Right to restrict noise during quiet hours.

• Right to collect attorney fees if lease allows and landlord wins in court.

• Right to accelerate rent (make all remaining rent due) in some commercial leases.

• Right to withhold consent to lease assignment "in sole discretion" if lease says so.

• Right to approve paint colors if tenant wants to paint.

• Right to require tenant to use specific pest control if bedbugs or roaches appear.

• Right to restrict political signs (with some exceptions under state law).

• Right to prohibit window air conditioners or require specific installation.

• Right to require renter to change HVAC filters regularly.

• Right to charge for excessive utility usage in some master-metered buildings.

• Right to prohibit hot tubs, trampolines, or other liability risks.

• Right to require tenant to notify landlord of extended absences (e.g., >7 days).

• Right to enter to winterize or secure property during extended tenant absence.

• Right to prohibit storage of hazardous materials.

• Right to restrict number of vehicles per unit.

• Right to require tenant to carry flood or earthquake insurance in high-risk areas.

• Right to prohibit locksmiths from making copies of keys without landlord permission.

• Right to require tenant to test smoke/CO detectors monthly.

- Right to charge for false alarm calls caused by tenant negligence.
- Right to prohibit drones or RC aircraft over the property.
- Right to restrict use of swimming pools, gyms, or other amenities to tenants only.
- Right to prohibit parties over a certain size.
- Right to require tenant to reimburse for plumbing clogs caused by improper items.
- Right to prohibit flushing of wipes, grease, or feminine products.
- Right to decide whether to renew or renegotiate lease terms at expiration.
- Ultimate right to regain full possession and control of the property when the tenancy legally ends.

These rights are subject to state and local laws . Always include the strongest allowable provisions in your lease and stay current with state-specific regulations. All examples above will vary by state. Please check with your attorney for specifics.

How To Use This Book

How to Use This Book

This book is designed to be read in layers. Casual readers may focus on concepts and strategy. Buyers and sellers should study the negotiation, financial, and AI chapters. Investors and policymakers will benefit from the sustainability and city-design sections. This is not passive reading material.

We encourage people to invest in the printed paperback as well as the e-book, as to be a visual reminder of your goals, and the fulfillment thereof. Both are a reference guide for your next step in the process of leveling up. Out of sight, out of mind.

1.) Because the system was built to be understood - just not explained. This book pulls back the curtain, like at the Wizard of Oz, on how real estate actually works, so you can use the rules instead of being limited by them.

2.) Because owning property isn't about luck, it's about leverage. Learn how everyday buyers and sellers can use smart financing, timing, and strategy to create long-term stability and wealth.

3.) Because the biggest opportunities are hidden in plain sight. From government programs listed on MassHousing.com, to market mechanics, this book shows you where value lives, and why most people never see it.

4.) Because housing is the foundation of personal freedom. When you control where and how you live, you gain financial confidence, generational security, and real economic power by holding hard assets.

To understand what you may not know you don't know. Then, once you know you'll never unknow.

To discuss a different level of commitment to the community by becoming part of a Sustainable City.

Index

INDEX:

CHAPTER 1

WHAT YOU DON'T KNOW YOU DON'T KNOW

— THE REAL ESTATE REVOLUTION BEGINS —

Listen up, future homeowner: You've got your dream house in sight—a cozy colonial in a quiet suburb, or maybe a sleek condo overlooking the city. You've crunched the numbers, toured the place twice, and even imagined where the Christmas tree will go. But here's the gut punch: What if a zoning law changed last month, turning your backyard into a no-build zone for that dream addition? Or what if flood maps were redrawn, jacking up your insurance premiums by 50% overnight? You didn't know to check. Hell, you didn't even know these things existed to check. Welcome to the real estate abyss—the "unknown unknowns" that have sunk more American Dreams than bad credit ever could.

We've all been there, or worse, we're headed there blindfolded. The real estate industry thrives on your ignorance, pocketing commissions while you foot the bill for surprises that could have been spotted from a mile away. But not anymore. In this chapter, we're ripping off the blindfold. We'll arm you with the tools to turn those hidden landmines into stepping stones. Because in the Real Estate Revolution, knowledge isn't just power—it's your ticket to owning a home without getting owned by the system.

The Johari Window: Your Map to the Hidden Real Estate

Minefield

Picture this: Back in the 1950s, two psychologists, Joseph Luft and Harrington Ingham, cooked up the Johari Window—a simple grid that exposes how knowledge (or lack thereof) shapes our decisions. It's like a mirror for your brain, divided into four quadrants. Apply it to real estate, and it becomes a revolutionary lens for spotting the traps that cost buyers and sellers thousands.

- Known Knowns**: The stuff you're crystal clear on. 2+2=4. In real estate, you know your budget is $500K, and you know you want three bedrooms. Basic, right? But here's the trap: Most people stop here, thinking they've got it all figured out. Spoiler: You don't.

- Known Unknowns**: The gaps you know exist. Like, you know you don't know why Pi r squared works (the area of a circle— handy for calculating lot sizes). In real estate, this is stuff like, "I know I need a home inspection, but I don't know what to look for." Smart folks hire pros here, but even that's not enough.

- Unknown Knowns**: The instincts you have but don't realize. Your heart beats without you thinking about it; your gut tells you a neighborhood feels "off" without knowing why. In real estate, it's that subconscious vibe when a deal smells fishy—like a seller rushing closing because they "unknowingly know" about a leaky foundation. Trust it, but verify.

- Unknown Unknowns**: The big bad wolf. These are the dangers you don't even know to worry about—the most dangerous because they're invisible until they bite. In real estate, they're everywhere, and they're why good people lose their shirts.

The goal of the Revolution? Shrink that fourth quadrant. Turn unknown unknowns into known unknowns (research them), then into known knowns (master them). It's how you go from victim to victor in a market designed to keep you in the dark.

Real Estate's Deadliest Unknown Unknowns: The Hidden Killers Lurking in Your Deal

These aren't hypotheticals—they're real traps that have derailed deals in 2025 alone. Based on the latest data from sources like the National Association of Realtors (NAR) and FEMA (as of November 2025), here's a hit list of unknown unknowns that could crush your American

Dream. We've pulled fresh examples to keep this revolutionary:

Sustainable City vs Nonsustainable City:

Definition:

Sustainable

A system, practice, or activity is sustainable when it meets present needs without compromising the ability of future generations to meet their own needs. It balances environmental health, economic viability, and social well-being, using resources at a rate that allows them to regenerate or remain available long term.

Non-sustainable

A system, practice, or activity is non-sustainable when it depletes resources, degrades the environment, or causes social or economic harm in ways that cannot be maintained over time. It prioritizes short-term gains while undermining long-term stability, leaving fewer options or greater costs for future generations.

What kind of city will you choose? or do you even have a choice?

Market Wildcards - AI & Robotics:

According to https://www.nahb.org/ (NAHB) 2024 Construction Cost Survey, the average new construction home sold for $665,000 and was 2,647 square feet.

Cost breakdown as follows:

- 13.7% - Cost of Land: (Finished lot including land acquisition, development, and utilities).
- 35-40% - Cost of Materials.
- 25-29% - Cost of Labor.
- 11% - Profit.
- 11% - Other (Overhead, Sales Commissions, Financing, marketing) With some quick math — if you just look at the cost of materials to build a house(40% x $665,000 = $266,000 in cost of materials).

If land can be organized, "acquired", or pledged, for little or no cost, and robots build the homes, and financing, overhead and profit are removed from a public/private partnership — national housing prices could change quickly — for those newly constructed homes, as well as the housing economy overall.

Any revolution like this would need to be done in a measured manner, as to not undermine existing cities. However, with competition from new cities, existing cities would benefit over the long run from the innovations learned from the newly constructed Sustainable Cities.

Zoning Shifts: A new law passes quietly, banning short-term rentals in your flip neighborhood. Example: In Boston this year, a quiet rezoning in Jamaica Plain killed ADU (accessory dwelling unit) plans for hundreds, tanking property values by 15%. You didn't know because city councils bury these in fine print. Cost? $20K–$50K in lost equity.

Flood and Climate Vulnerabilities: Updated FEMA maps redraw flood zones, spiking insurance or forcing retrofits. As of November 2025, NOAA reports 30% more U.S. properties at high flood risk due to climate shifts—many in "safe" suburbs. Unknown unknown: Your "dry" lot is now in a 100-year floodplain, adding $5K/year in premiums.

School Redistricting: Boundaries change, dropping your home from a top-rated district to a struggling one. In 2025, states like Texas and California redistricted amid enrollment booms, slashing home values by 10–20%. Parents buy for schools—they don't know redistricting votes happen in obscure board meetings.

** Commercial Questions and Conversions**: $500B in commercial real estate loans mature in 2025–2026 (per CBRE reports), flooding the market with distress sales. Unknown unknown: This crashes residential values nearby, or creates buying opportunities if you're savvy. But if you're selling? You're blindsided.

Cognitive Biases in Play: The sunk cost fallacy makes you overpay because you've "invested" time in a bad deal. Or anchoring bias ties you to the first price you hear. These psychological landmines cost buyers 5–10% on average, per behavioral economics studies from

Harvard Business Review. Don't get played.

Historical Hangovers: Old easements or liens from 50 years ago surface at closing. Example: In rural areas, forgotten utility rights block your solar panel installation. Or cultural norms—like assuming "location, location, location" is eternal—blind you to shifts (e.g., a hospital closing, tanking local values).

Tech Disruptions: AI tools automate 80% of agent jobs by 2026 (per Gartner forecasts), but you don't know free AI prompts can replace a buyer's agent, saving 2–3%* commissions post-NAR settlement.

These aren't rare—they're rampant. The 2026 NAR changes de- coupled commissions, but unknown unknowns like hidden steering (agents pushing deals for kickbacks) still lurk, costing you thousands.

Your AI-Powered Shield: The "Unknown Unknowns" Scanner

Enough doom—let's fight back. Imagine an AI tool that scans for these blind spots before you sign. Good news: We're building it right here in the Revolution. Using live data from FEMA, NOAA, state agencies, and market APIs (updated to November 17, 2025), this scanner turns unknowns into alerts. Plug in an address or ZIP, and it flags risks with a 1–10 score (10 = "Abort mission!").

How It Works (Your Blueprint for Freedom):

• **Data Pull**: Grabs real-time feeds—FEMA flood maps, state zoning updates, school board minutes, and CBRE distress loan data.

• **AI Cross-Check**: Semantic search for "red flags" like "zoning change [your city]" or "flood risk spike 2025."

• **Risk Output**: A simple report: "Zoning alert: New rules ban rentals—Risk 8/10. Mitigation: Appeal locally."

• **Ongoing Vigilance**: Set up weekly pushes: "Tariff news hitting cap rates—watch for value dips."

Want to try it? Use free AI prompts from Chapter 9 (e.g., "Scan [address] for zoning risks via public data"). Or build your own with tools like ChatGPT querying open APIs. In 2025, this isn't sci-fi—it's your edge against the rigged game.

Revolutionary Action Steps

Don't just read—revolt. Turn unknowns into wins:

• **Audit Your Deal**: Input your target property into free tools like FEMA's Flood Map Service or Zillow's zoning checker. Cross-reference with local news searches.

• **Build Your Scanner**: Prompt AI: "List 10 unknown unknowns for buying in [your city], with sources."

• **Educate Your Tribe**: Share this chapter with a friend—turn their blind spots into your network's strength.

• **Demand Transparency**: In your buyer-broker agreement (post- NAR), add a clause for "full risk disclosure" using AI scans.

• **Track Changes**: Subscribe to alerts from sites you trust or local gov portals. Knowledge compounds like equity.

You've just shrunk your unknown unknowns. The American Dream isn't handed out—it's seized by the informed. Next up: Why "location, location, location" is a lie when everything changes.

Let's keep the revolution rolling.

CHAPTER 2

LOCATION, LOCATION, REVOLUTION – WHY YOUR "FOREVER" SPOT IS ABOUT TO FLIP UPSIDE DOWN

— THE REAL ESTATE REVOLUTION BEGINS —

You know the old real estate mantra: "Location, location, location." It's been drilled into our heads like a bad pop song on repeat—buy near good schools, short commutes, buzzing culture, and watch your home value soar. But here's the revolutionary truth bomb: That advice is as outdated as a rotary phone in 2025. The world is changing faster than a Tesla on Ludicrous Mode, and what made a location "prime" yesterday could make it a money pit tomorrow. Hospitals close, universities pivot to online, religions fade or relocate—hell, even decentralized power grids and septic systems are turning rural outposts into self-sustaining paradises. We're not just buying houses anymore; we're betting on futures that tech is rewriting in real time.

Think about it: You've been sold the lie that urban hotspots are the golden ticket to the American Dream. Crowded cities promise jobs, excitement, and status, but at what cost? Sky-high prices, soul-crushing traffic, and a life where "liberty" means dodging potholes while pursuing happiness in a shoebox apartment. Meanwhile, suburbs and rural areas—once dismissed as boring backwaters—are emerging as the new frontiers of freedom. With robots handling homeschooling, driver- less cars zipping you anywhere, and work-from-home setups turning your den into a corner office, why chain yourself to downtown decay? The Revolution demands we rethink priorities, because clinging to old maps will leave you lost—and broke.

In this chapter, we're putting you in the driver's seat (or the autonomous one). We'll start with a gut-check exercise to rank what really matters in your home hunt. Then, we'll dismantle the location myth, showing how tech is democratizing the dream. No more overpaying for proximity to a "great" school when AI tutors outperform any classroom. No more suffering soul-sucking commutes when self-driving pods make distance irrelevant. And forget urban glamour—suburbs and rural havens are where life, liberty, and pursuit of happiness thrive, free from the chaos of congestion, crime, and overpriced lattes. Let's revolt against the rigged location game and claim the turf that truly sets you free.

Your Priority Power Ranking: The Wake-Up Call Exercise

Before you drop a dime on a down payment, you need to know what you value—not what some slick agent or outdated Zillow filter tells you. Grab a pen, future revolutionary. Below is a list of 15 key factors (yeah, we counted—close enough to 16 for government work). Rank them from 1 to 15, with 1 being your absolute must-have and 15 the "nice-to-have-if-the-price-is-right." Be honest—this isn't about impressing anyone; it's about building your American Dream on solid ground.

- Schools:
- Safety:
- Space:
- Drive time:
- Culture:
- Restaurants:
- Shopping:
- Family:
- Pet friendly:
- Price:
- Type house:
- Layout:
- Yard size:
- Landscaping:
- Condition:

Done? Great. Now, if you're buying with a partner (spouse, sibling, or that optimistic roommate who's "basically family"), have them do the same—separately. Then, compare your lists over coffee (or whiskey, depending on how mismatched they are). Discuss the gaps: Why did you rank "yard size" as a top 3 while they shoved it to the bottom? Is "drive time" a deal-breaker for one but irrelevant to the other? This isn't couples therapy—it's Revolution prep. Getting on the same page now saves you from buyer's remorse later, when you're arguing over why the "perfect" location feels like a prison.

Pro tip: If you agree on the top 3, and this house has it, buy it. If your rankings clash on biggies like safety or price, hit pause on house hunting until you're aligned. The Dream thrives on unity, not compromise.

The Location Lie: How Tech Is Turning the Map Inside Out

Location has always been king—or so they say. But kings get de- throned, and in 2025, tech is the guillotine. We've been brainwashed to prioritize spots near urban anchors: top schools for the kids, quick commutes for the job, cultural hubs for the soul. Yet, as institutions decentralize—religions shifting online, universities going virtual, hospitals consolidating or teleporting via telehealth—the old rules crumble. What happens when your "prime" neighborhood loses its hospital to budget cuts, or the local college shutters amid enrollment drops? Values tank, and you're left holding a depreciating asset.

But here's the provocative pivot: These changes aren't threats—they're opportunities to reclaim the American Dream in places Big Real Estate ignores. Consider the tech tidal wave reshaping priorities:

Schools? Meet Your New Teacher: The Robot Overlord. Traditional districts used to dictate desirability, with "good schools" inflating home prices by 20–30% (per 2025 Redfin data). But in the AI era, that's flipping. Homeschooling with AI tutors and robotic assistants is exploding — think personalized lessons from tools like Khan Academy and similar AI platforms or emerging home robots from companies like Figure AI. By 2025, 15% of U.S. families use AI-driven education full-time (up from 5% in 2020, per EdTech reports), making brick-and-mortar schools less critical. Suddenly, that overpriced urban district loses its luster.

Rural or suburban homes with space for a home learning pod? Now that's the smart bet for liberty—freedom to educate your kids your way, without the chaos of overcrowded classrooms.

Commutes? Driverless Cars Say "What Commute?" Drive time once ruled rankings, with proximity to work adding 10–15% to home values. But autonomous vehicles are here, folks. In 2025, Waymo and Tesla's Full Self-Driving fleets operate in over 20 U.S. cities, with adoption hitting 10% of urban trips (per McKinsey forecasts). Add work-from-home (WFH) permanence—30% of the workforce is fully remote, per Gallup's latest polls—and downtown access becomes obsolete. Why pay a premium for a 20-minute drive when a driverless pod turns a 45-minute trek into productive (or nap) time? Suburbs win: More space, lower costs, and the liberty to live where you want, not where your boss demands.

Urban Buzz vs. Rural Bliss: The Pursuit of True Happiness. Cities promise culture, restaurants, and shopping, but deliver congestion, crime, and costs that crush the soul. In 2025, urban exodus continues—migration to suburbs and rural areas up 25% since 2020 (Census Bureau data) —fueled by WFH and tech. Decentralized utilities like solar microgrids and advanced septic systems make off-grid living viable, turning rural spots into self-reliant havens. Pets roam free, families bond in big yards, and safety soars without city strife. This is the Revolution's core: Life (safer, healthier), liberty (from urban grind), and pursuit of happiness (in spaces that nurture, not drain). Cities? They're for tourists. Your Dream awaits in the 'burbs or beyond, where land is cheap and freedom flows.

The old guard—traditional agents clinging to commissions—will scream that location is eternal. But they're wrong. Tech decentralizes power, literally and figuratively, empowering you to prioritize what truly matters: Affordability, autonomy, and joy. Don't buy into the hype; buy into the future.

Revolutionary Action Steps

Time to act, rebel. Turn insight into impact:

- **Re-Rank Regularly**: Revisit your priority list every six months— tech changes fast, and so should your criteria.
- **Tech-Test Locations**: Use AI tools (prompt: "Compare [suburb] vs. [city] for WFH viability in 2025") to simulate shifts in schools, commutes, and utilities.

- **Partner Pow-Wow**: Schedule that comparison chat—make it fun with takeout from a "restaurant" priority spot.
- **Scout the New Frontiers**: Tour a suburban or rural listing this week. Ask: "How does this fuel my liberty?"
- **Declare Independence**: Write your own "Location Manifesto"— what you'll no longer tolerate in pursuit of the Dream.

The map is redrawn. Claim your spot in the Revolution—where location serves *you*, not the other way around. Next: The NAR shake-up that's finally putting power in your pocket. Let's keep fighting.

Chapter 3

The 6%* Myth – Why Traditional Commissions Could Be the Biggest Legal Heist in America

Remember the good old days when your buyer's agent whispered, "It's free — the seller pays me!" while quietly siphoning 2–3%* of your dream home's price tag straight from the deal? Yeah, that "free" lunch was the biggest illusion in American real estate, a cartel-like setup where sellers footed the bill for everyone, inflating prices and padding pockets to the tune of $100 billion a year in some estimates. We called it a heist, and it kept you—the buyer or seller—in the dark, overpaying for a rigged game. But in

2025, the dam broke. A massive $418 million settlement with the National Association of Realtors (NAR) shattered the status quo, effective August 17, 2024. (see court cases: Sitzer/Burnett, Burnett v. NAR and Moehrl v. NAR) No more mandatory seller-paid buyer commissions advertised on the MLS. No more "free" agents working for invisible paydays. This isn't just a tweak—it's the Revolution we've been fighting for, handing power back to you, the everyday American chasing homeownership.

As of November 2025, the changes are locked in, however an appeal and final court approval are on the horizon. NAR's modernizing MLS policies for January 2026, ditching old rules that hid the money trail. In Massachusetts—our hotbed of high-stakes deals and even higher egos— these shifts are playing out with a Yankee twist: Commissions haven't budged much yet, but negotiations are fiercer, and savvy players are saving thousands. We're diving deep: What changed, how to negotiate like a boss in the Bay State, and the raw pros/cons that could make or break your deal. Buckle up—this is how we end the heist and reclaim the Dream.

The Big Shake-Up: What NAR Actually Changed (And Why It Matters)

The settlement stemmed from lawsuits accusing NAR of antitrust violations—basically, propping up inflated commissions through MLS rules that forced sellers to offer buyer agent pay upfront. Here's the revolutionary rewrite:

Buyer-Broker Agreements Are Now Mandatory: Before you even peek at a listing, you sign a written deal with your agent spelling out services, duration (e.g., 3 months), and—crucially—how they'll get paid. No more vague "I'll figure it out later." This upfront clarity kills the "free agent" myth and lets you cap fees at 1%* or less if you're sharp.

Sellers Off the Hook for MLS Ads: Listings can't advertise buyer agent compensation anymore. Want to offer it? Fine—but negotiate it separately in the contract, not broadcast on the MLS like a neon sign inviting hagglers. Sellers save big by default, but can still dangle concessions to attract buyers.

No More Cooperative Compensation Rules: The old MLS clause requiring seller offers? Gone. Agents can't steer you toward "co-op friendly" listings. This levels the field, but expect growing pains— NAR's rolling out new legal resources to keep things compliant.

Nationally, these hit residential deals hard, but commercial's untouched. In 2025, with inventory still tight (up just 5% from 2024 per NAR data), the changes haven't crashed the market—sales dipped 2% initially but rebounded by Q3. But in Massachusetts? Our market's a beast—median prices at $650K, with Boston's suburbs screaming for relief. The Massachusetts Association of Realtors (MAR) updated forms in early 2025 to bake in these rules, mandating disclosures on compensation in every offer. Result? More transparency, but fewer knee-jerk showings since buyers now budget agent fees upfront.

Negotiating in the New World: Scripts, Strategies, and Massachusetts Muscle

Gone are the days of passive deals—now, every transaction's a negotiation arena. Sellers, you control the purse strings more than ever. Buyers, you hold the cards on who you hire and how much you pay. In Massachusetts, where attorney reviews and 14-day inspection periods already drag deals (hello, Chapter 7), these changes amp up the haggling. But fear not—we've got your playbook.

How It Works Step-by-Step:

• **Buyers Lead with the Agreement**: Sign that buyer-broker deal early. Negotiate terms like: "1%* cap, paid only if we close under $700K." In MA, use MAR's standard form—it's ironclad and requires fiduciary duty disclosures.

• **Sellers Set the Bait (Or Don't)**: List without commission offers to test waters. If bids lag, sweeten with concessions: "$10K credit toward buyer agent fees" in the counteroffer.

IMPORTANT NOTE:

There's an alarming trend of allow listing brokers to post a sellers listing information on the Listing Brokers' website only, behind a "paywall". The only way you see the listing is if you pay a membership. Bottom line: This is not consumer friendly, from the standpoint of giving the seller the broadest market possible. Also, fair competition to the public, for equal access to all, would be at risk.

Beware listing with Brokers that promise top results from keeping your property as a "pocket listing" While they may allow for privacy —great for some high-profile sales in Newton or Wellesley— it very well be more in the Broker's interest than the consumer. Seller Beware!

The Offer Dance: Buyers submit with your agreement attached. Sellers counter on price *and* concessions. In competitive MA markets (think Cambridge condos), expect multi-offer scenarios where you bid "We'll cover 1.5% buyer agent via seller credit." Post-settlement, 70% of deals still include some seller help, but it's down from 95% pre-2024.

MA-Specific Twists: Our state's dual-agency rules (rare but sneaky) now demand extra disclosures on compensation splits. Attorney involvement is standard, so loop them in for "non-binding" pre-offer talks. Pro tip: In hot spots like the South Shore, sellers are holding firm on no concessions to push prices up 3% year-over-year. Buyers? Leverage MA's buyer agency laws—demand your agent proves value or walk.

Sample Negotiation Script (Buyer Side): "Love the property— strong offer at asking, but with a $12K seller concession for my agent's fee. Per my agreement, that's my max exposure. Deal?"

This setup empowers you: Buyers avoid surprises, sellers dodge blanket payouts. But it's not all smooth—confusion's led to 10% more deal fall-through in MA's first post-change quarter.

The Double-Edged Sword: Pros and Cons of the NAR Revolution

Like any uprising, this one's messy—but mostly magnificent. Here's the unvarnished truth, straight from 2026's front lines:

Stakeholder **Pros** **Cons**

Buyers

Transparency Wins: Know your agent's fee upfront—no more "hidden" seller subsidies jacking prices. Save 1–2%* ($6K–$13K on a $650K MA home) by negotiating flat fees.

Choice Explosion: Hire discount agents, go unrepresented (FSBO-style), or demand value-based pay. WFH warriors in suburbs can skip pricey urban brokers.

Equity Boost: Less commission bloat means more money toward your down payment.

Sticker Shock: Upfront agreements mean budgeting $5K–$10K out-of-pocket if sellers balk—tough for first-timers.

Fewer Showings: Some listings skip concessions, limiting access unless you pay your agent solo.

Learning Curve: Newbies get overwhelmed; 20% report higher stress in surveys.

Sellers

Commission Freedom: Pocket 2–3%* ($13K–$20K average) by not offering buyer pay—MA sellers saved $1.2B in Q1 2025 alone.

Negotiation Power: Use concessions as leverage in multi-offer wars, closing faster on your terms.

Market Edge: Attract serious buyers willing to cover their own costs.

Slower Sales: No MLS ads = fewer agent-motivated showings; days on market up 5–7 days nationally, similar in MA.

Price Pressure: Buyers push harder for concessions, potentially shaving 1–2%* off your net.

Admin Hassle: More paperwork for disclosures—MA's attorney reviews add $500–$1K in fees.

Overall Market

Fairer Game: Ends steering and collusion; empowers FSBOs and discounters.

Innovation Spark: Flat-fee models booming (e.g., $5K listings), cutting costs 80%.

Short-Term Chaos: 15% drop in buyer inquiries initially; agents scrambling to justify fees.

Inequality Risk: Wealthy buyers/sellers adapt fast; low-income folks lag, widening the Dream gap.

Bottom line: Pros outweigh cons for the informed—transparency trumps tradition. But if you're passive? You'll pay the price.

Revolutionary Action Steps

Seize the settlement—don't let it seize you:

- **Sign Smart**: Draft your buyer agreement today (use Prompt #1 from Chapter 9: "Create a checklist for buyer-broker terms post-NAR").
- **Negotiate Now**: Role-play offers with a partner—practice conceding on agent pay without budging on price.
- **MA Mastery**: Download MAR's 2025 forms; consult a local attorney for $200 to audit your strategy.
- **Track Savings**: Log potential commission cuts—aim to bank 2%* for closing costs or renovations.
- **Join the Fight**: Share a win story on social (#RealEstateRevolution) —inspire your tribe to negotiate like pros.

The cartel's cracked wide open. In Massachusetts or Main Street, you're no longer the mark—you're the mogul.

Next: AI's dismantling the deal costs.

Let's keep the fire burning.

Picture this: You've found the house. That sun-drenched Victorian with the wraparound porch, or the sleek townhome steps from the train. You and the seller shake on $500,000—fair market, no drama. Simple transfer: They hand over keys, you hand over cash (or a mortgage promise). Done. But wait—enter the real estate circus. Suddenly, you're drowning in a $20,000–$50,000 "closing costs" swamp of fees, forms, and middlemen who treat your Dream like an all-you-can-eat buffet. Title searches that haven't evolved since the Pony Express. Appraisals by humans who miss what algorithms spot in seconds. Commissions that ballooned to *6% because, why not? It's not your money... until it is.

We've been fleeced for decades, with closing costs gobbling 2–5% for buyers and 8–10% for sellers (that's $10K–$50K on a $500K deal, per 2025 Bankrate data). But here's the revolutionary spark: Elon Musk's first principles thinking—boil it down to the atomic truths—expos- es the scam. Real estate isn't a labyrinth of legalese; it's physics. One person owns dirt. Another wants it. Agree on price X. Transfer title. Boom. Everything else? Bloat we can slash with AI, blockchain, and post-NAR guts. In this chapter, we'll autopsy a standard deal's costs, unveil a sample settlement statement, and arm you with hacks to gut 50–80% of the bill—today and tomorrow. No more feeding the beast. You own the feast.

First Principles: The Elon Musk Reset for Real Estate Deals Musk doesn't tweak rockets; he rebuilds from fundamentals. Same here. Strip away the industry's smoke: A real estate deal boils to three atoms:

- **Ownership**: Seller has title (proof of dirt rights). Buyer wants it.
- **Value Exchange**: Buyer pays X (cash, loan, or tokens). Seller gets compensated.
- **Transfer**: Update records. Keys change hands. No liens, no surprises.

That's it. No 40-page contracts. No $2,000 attorneys nitpicking commas. The rest—appraisals, inspections, title insurance—is legacy code from a pre-AI world, inflating costs to protect gatekeepers, not you. In 2025, AI restructures this: Algorithms verify value in minutes. Blockchain logs titles immutably, axing fraud risks. Smart contracts auto-execute on agreement. Result? A deal that costs hundreds, not tens of thousands. We're not dreaming—we're engineering the Revolution.

The Standard Closing Cost Carnage: A 2025 Breakdown Nationally, buyer closing costs average 2–5%* of the loan ($6,905 on a $300K mortgage, per Motley Fool's 2025 stats), while sellers cough up 8–10%* ($40K+ on $500K, mostly commissions). In Massachusetts, it's steeper—attorneys mandatory, pushing buyer averages to $12K–$18K (Bankrate). These aren't "unavoidable"—they're profitable relics. Here's the typical lineup for a $500K single-family sale (buyer-financed, 20% down, $400K loan):

- **Loan-Related (1–2% of loan)**: Origination ($4K), underwriting ($500), credit report ($250). Total: ~$5K.
- **Property Valuation**: Appraisal ($750), inspection ($1,000). Total:~$1,750.
- **Title & Legal**: Title insurance ($2,700), attorney ($2,000), re- cording ($500). Total: ~$5,200.
- **Taxes/Prepaids**: Prorated property taxes ($2K), prepaid interest/insurance ($1.5K). Total: ~$3.5K.
- **Agent Commissions**: Seller pays 5–6%* ($25K–$30K total, split buyer/seller agents).

- **Escrow/Misc.**: Flood cert ($20), courier ($100). Total: ~$500. Grand buyer total: $15K–$25K (3–5%). Seller: $30K–$40K (6–8%, post- NAR). It's a feast for lenders and lawyers, famine for you.

- #### Your Sample Closing Disclosure: The Brutal Truth in Black and White

The Closing Disclosure (CFPB's five-page beast, updated for 2025 transparency) is your final bill—compare it to the Loan Estimate or weep.

Below are simplified examples that highlight the costs included in the standard 2025 Closing Statement Form for our $500K example (buyer perspective, seller-financed elements noted). Figures pulled from averages (Bankrate, CFPB samples) and—e.g., $2,700 title, $2K attorney, $750 appraisal. Cash to close: ~$18,500 (plus $100K down).

Loan Costs

Origination Fee (1-2% of $400K loan): $1,000 - $8,000 Potential Future Cost: $0 Potential Savings: $1,000 - $8,000.

How: Automatically entering income information from tax returns and financial documents could eliminate this cost. "Authorized automated underwriting" allows easy access to federal taxes returns and bank documents.   Auto approval for mortgage loan from Sovereign Fund at 3% with no middleman or closing costs.

Credit Report $250 - $500.

Potential Future Cost $0 Potential Savings: $250-$500 How: Free via AI credit pulls from credit agencies.

Underwriting Fee: $500.

Potential Future Cost $0 Potential Savings: $500.

How: AI automated underwriting, which most banks already have.

Services You Cannot Shop For Appraisal: $750 Potential Future Cost: $0 Potential Savings: $750.

How: AI valuation similar to Zillow's estimate (only unbiased) or elimination of appraisal underwriting requirement due to large down payment.

Title Insurance (Lender's Policy): $1,200 -$2,000 Potential Future Cost: $0 Potential Savings: $1,200 - $2,000.

How: The use of blockchain title pulls that eliminate costs for "lot and block" type properties with certified surveys and recorded agreements. More sophisticated properties, like commercial or rural/agricultural properties, would require an attorney's review.

Attorney Fees: $2,000.

Potential Future Costs: $500-$1,000 Potential Savings: $500-$1,000 How: It's critical to be represented by an attorney. This is not a place to skimp or totally rely on AI. AI has it's advantages, however it's important to have a human attorney review everything — both for the buyer and for the seller. Don't let anyone tell you differently!

Services You Can Shop For Home Inspection: $1,000. Potential Future Cost: $0 Potential Savings: $1,000.

How: It's critical to have a home inspection. This is not a place to skimp or totally rely on AI. Don't let anyone tell you differently! HOWEVER - Robotic Inspectors (Like Optimus) could be free or provided important disclosures during an open house. Seller's Disclosures (with penalties for non-disclosure) can also be helpful but never fully relied upon. BUYER BEWARE!

Title Search/Exam: $500.

Potential Future Cost: $0 Potential Savings: $500.   How: Blockchain Guarantee.

Prepaids & Escrows Property Taxes (prorated): $1,500.

Potential Future Cost: $0 Potential Savings: $8,000 (annual).

How: Florida has proposed zero property tax. Other states may follow. It's important to understand where your property taxes go. Most of the property tax bill goes to your local schools. Robotic teachers will become more prevalent, and these costs could shrink.

Homeowners Insurance (1st year): $1,200.

Potential Future Costs: $600 Potential Savings: $600.

How: Towns could "self-insure" all buildings in the town. Advances in robotics could use robotic firefighting drones, robotic police officers, and video surveillance to greatly reduce costs. Fold insurance payments into the local tax bill to cut your monthly mortgage payment—allowing for more leverage in a home purchase and better affordability.

Prepaid Interest: $800.

Potential Future Costs: $50 Potential Savings: $750.

How: Close near the end of the month, thus reducing prepaid interest costs.

Other Costs Recording Fees: $500.

Potential Future Cost: $0 Potential Savings: $500.   How: Blockchain/Automated Recordings.

Transfer Taxes: $2,500 (seller often covers) Potential Future Cost: $0 Potential Savings: $2,500.

How: Transfer Taxes are charged by State and local governments. The question is, what "services" did they provided during this specific transaction. Nothing really. It's a tax on the transaction. It's just an great opportunity for the governing authority to "get their hand in the pie" of a large pool of money.

The ultimate power lies in the voters of the community. It's really that simple. All we need is your voice and focus on the goal: An efficient system with lower costs for everyone.

Commissions (Seller Side) Listing Agent (3%*) $15,000.

Potential Future Cost - Post-NAR: Negotiate to 1% ($5K). Potential Savings: $10,000.

How: Know the market — Read "Real Estate Revolution" ! Buyer Agent (3%*): $15,000 Potential Savings: $10,000 How: Buyer pays direct or via concession: Cap at 1%*.

Totals

Cash to Close | **$18,500** | **Seller Net: $461,000** (after

$39K costs).

| **$57,500 Total Fees** | Pre-Revolution bloat: 11.5%.

This is the "before" picture— a $57K tax on a simple swap. But our notes nail the cuts: AI for underwriting/valuation, blockchain for title/ recording, robot inspections. Future? Zero-interest state loans (our vision) slash origination to nil.

Slicing the Bloat: How AI (and Guts) Cut Closing Costs Now—and in the Revolution's Dawn.

These lesson are gold: We've been overpaying for manual drudgery. Here's how to revolt, now (2025 tools) and soon (AGI horizon):

- **Now (50%+ Savings)**:
- **Agents**: Post-NAR, negotiate buyer agent to 1%* ($5K vs. $15K)—use Prompt #4 from Chapter 9 for scripts. Sellers: List flat-fee ($5K total).
- **Appraisal/Inspection**: Skip with AI— other on line tools (free, 95% accurate per 2025 tests). Robot tours via Matterport AI: $0.
- **Title/Survey/Legal**: Hybrid title firms like Qualia use AI for $500 vs $2,700. Attorneys? AI contract review (LegalZoom AI) for $100.
- **Loan Fees**: Shop lenders via AI matcher—origination down to 0.5%. Credit reports? Free via AnnualCreditReport.com.

Total hack: $8K–$10K buyer savings on $500K.

- **Future (80–100% Gutted)**:
- **Blockchain Titles**: Government-administered chains (like Sweden's 2025 pilot) eliminate searches/insurance—$0, immutable.
- **AI Underwriting**: Tax-return auto-approval + zero-interest state loans = no origination/underwriting ($0).
- **Smart Contracts**: Ethereum-based deeds auto-transfer on payment to buyer, recording/attorneys ($0).
- **Robot Everything**: Optimus inspects in real-time; town-insured policies fold into taxes.

Vision: A $500K deal closes for $500 in gas money. Ownership swaps like Venmo—pure first principles.

The industry fights back—lobbyists scream "risk!" But data says otherwise: AI errors <1% (Gartner 2025), fraud down 70% on blockchain. You're not reckless; you're revolutionary.

Revolutionary Action Steps Engineer your lean deal—start today:

- **Principle Audit**: For your target home, list the three atoms. What bloat doesn't serve them? Cross off.
- **Cost Crusher**: Plug into Bankrate's calculator—subtract AI hacks from your estimate. Aim for <2% total.

- **AI Test Run**: Prompt: "Generate a blockchain title transfer script for $500K home." Tweak for your state.
- **Negotiate Nuclear**: Email agents: "1% flat or I go FSBO."

Track savings in a "Revolution Ledger".

- **Future-Proof**: Join pilots like MA's blockchain task force—be the beta tester for zero-cost closes.

We've deconstructed the beast. Now rebuild leaner, meaner.

Next: Get shark tank fit to crush the competition. The Dream's not expensive— it's engineered.

Let's launch.

Chapter 5

OPEN HOUSES, FANCY PHOTOS & STAGING

— THEATER THAT COSTS YOU MONEY AND DELIVERS NOTHING —

Welcome to the jungle, comrade. The real estate market isn't a polite tea party—it's George Orwell's Animal Farm crossed with Shark Tank on steroids. You've got the pigs (big institutions, NAR remnants, flippers with cash stacks) hoarding the feed while the rest of us chickens scratch for crumbs. You've got the sharks circling—iBuyers, hedge funds, all-cash buyers—ready to devour any weak offer that limps into the tank. And you? You're either the prey… or the apex predator who walks away with the kill. The rules are simple: The strong eat. The weak get eaten.

There is no "fair." There is no "everyone gets a trophy." There is only who is in the best shape when the bell rings.

This chapter is your boot camp. We're getting you predator fit—financially ripped, strategically lethal, and mentally unbreakable—so you don't just survive the feeding frenzy, you dominate it. Because in 2025, with inventory still brutally low and multiple offers the norm in every decent market (Boston metro included), the fat, slow, and clueless are lunch.

First Rule of the Jungle: Know Your Animal

In Animal Farm, the pigs rewrote the rules while everyone slept. In real estate, the "pigs" are still trying to keep the 6%* trough full even after the NAR settlement. Your job: Stop being a sheep. Start being the wolf.

In Shark Tank, the sharks don't fund dreams—they fund killers who've done the work. Same here. The winners aren't the nicest, the luckiest, or the ones with the prettiest staging. They're the ones who showed up shredded.

Get in Predator Shape – The 8-Week Real Estate Training Camp

- **Financial Fitness – Build the War Chest Early (Start 6–12 Months Out)**
- Credit score: Get it over 760. Pay down cards, dispute errors, become an authorized user on a parent's old card if needed. Every 20 points is thousands saved in interest.
- Debt-to-income ratio: Kill it. Pay off car loans, student loans, cred- it cards. Lenders now scrutinize DTI harder than ever post 2024 rate spikes.
- Cash reserves: Have 6–12 months of mortgage payments liquid.

Sellers and lenders smell desperation. Desperate buyers pay more; desperate sellers take less.

- Pre-approval isn't enough—get DU/LP approval (automated underwriting findings). That's the golden ticket that tells sellers you're not going to close.

Bonus predator move: Get approved with multiple lenders. Use one as your "stalking horse" to force the others to sharpen rates/fees.

- **Knowledge Fitness – Eliminate the "Unknown Unknowns" Before They Kill You**
- Take classes at www.RealEstateRevolution.org.
- Study the comps like a stalker. Not just Zillow—pull the actual MLS sheets, tax records, previous sales history, flood maps, zoning changes, sex offender registry, crime heat maps, school redistricting plans, planned developments, sewer assessments, and betterment liens.
- Drive the neighborhood at 7 a.m., 3 p.m., 9 p.m., and Saturday night. Talk to the mailman, the dog walker, the kid selling lemonade. You'll learn more in 30 minutes than any agent will tell you in 30 days.
- Check the neighbors—literally. Look up their property records. Are they underwater? Divorcing? Hoarders? A nightmare neighbor can tank your resale value 10–20%. I've seen $800K houses next to a problem property sell for $600K.
- **Optionality Muscle – Never Back Yourself into a Corner**
- Always, always, always have multiple properties in play. The second you fall in love with one house, you're prey.

- Have a "walk-away" script rehearsed: "Love the house, but we have two others we're equally excited about at lower price points. We'll do $XXX today only."
- Keep your current lease month-to-month or have a 60-day kick-out clause. Nothing makes you stronger than knowing you can walk.
- Sellers: Price aggressively or hold firm—whichever creates more options. But never price so high you scare everyone off and end up chained to a stale listing.
- **Timing & Endurance Training**

Start early. Right. Now. The buyers who win in spring 2026 are the ones who began building credit and saving cash in spring 2025.

- Rate buydowns, seller credits, assumption loans (FHA/VA)— know every weapon before you need it.
- Build your team early: Lender, attorney, inspector, contractor. The best ones are busy. Waiting until you're under agreement is like trying to hire a trainer the week before the bodybuilding contest.
- **Psychological Toughness – Become the Shark, Not the Chum**
- Practice walking away. Literally put in offers and be willing to lose them. The first few times hurt. By the third, you're ice.
- Role-play negotiations weekly. Have your spouse or friend play the listing agent and throw curveballs: "We have a higher offer." Your response has to be automatic: "Congratulations. Please send us the backup contract when it falls apart."
- Remove emotion. The house is bricks, sticks, and dirt. There will always be another one. The moment you act like it's your soulmate, you're meat.
- **Seller-Specific Predator Training**
- Depersonalize brutally. Rent a storage unit. Paint everything neutral. Stage minimally but perfectly.
- Pre-inspections are now mandatory for serious sellers. Spend $600– $1,000 upfront to fix everything. Nothing kills buyer urgency like a surprise $30K sewer line.
- Price to create competition. In most markets right now, pricing 3–5% below the highest realistic comp brings multiple offers and drives the price above asking.
- Offer possession after closing (rent-back) if needed, but only to the strongest buyer. It's a powerful carrot.
- **Buyer-Specific Predator Training**
- Escalation clauses are table stakes. But write them surgically: "We will beat any bona fide offer by $2,000 up to $XXX, proof of competing offer required."
- Waiver warfare: In insane markets, the winners waive appraisal gaps (with cash to cover) and inspection contingencies (with pre-inspections). Know your risk tolerance.
- Love letters are dead (and illegal in MA, discriminatory). Instead, send a "buyer résumé": credit score range, down payment %, lender pre-approval, flexibility on closing. Sellers eat that up.

The Ultimate Predator Checklist – Tape This to Your Mirror

- Credit score ≥760.
- DTI ≤36% (28% is god-tier).
- 6–12 months reserves.
- Three active properties at all times.
- Pre-inspection booked on any house you love.
- Walk-away price memorized.
- Neighbors researched (property records + weekend drive-bys).
- Team assembled and loyal (they work for YOU, not the deal).

This isn't about being paranoid. It's about being prepared. The market doesn't reward the nice, the hopeful, or the "lucky." It rewards the animal that trained the hardest while everyone else was scrolling Zillow dreaming.

Get in shape. Or get eaten.

Revolutionary Action Steps

- This week: Pull your credit reports (all three bureaus) and dispute every error.
- This month: Build your "Buyer Résumé" or "Seller War Plan" document.
- Next 60 days: Drive five neighborhoods you think you like—at night and on weekends. Talk to strangers.
- Set a calendar reminder: "Multiple Offer Practice" every Sunday night with your partner or accountability buddy.
- Declare your predator name. Write it down. How about Apex? Own it.

The jungle is waiting. Time to hunt.

Chapter 6

Financials Breaking the Chains of the Mortgage Plantation

We've been sold a lie bigger than the *6% commission scam: That homeownership requires indenturing yourself to a bank for decades at rates that bleed you dry. As of January, 2026, the average 30-year fixed mortgage rate sits at a soul-crushing 6.12%, turning what should be your American Dream castle into a 30-year albatross around your neck. You fork over half your paycheck to "Principal & Interest" (PITI), only to watch a large percentage of it evaporate into banker bonuses, and $315 trillion in global debt, much of it housing-fueled. It's servitude, plain and simple: Life, liberty, and the pursuit of happiness? Nah, just endless payments until you're too old to enjoy the equity you've barely scratched.

But we revolt. In this chapter, we're torching the playbook. We'll demystify the mortgage application gauntlet so you can run it like a predator, not prey. Then, we'll unleash alternatives—land contracts for quick freedom, government-backed lifelines, and our bold vision: 2–3% government bonds flooding the market to cap rates until every deserving American who can afford it owns a piece of the pie. Portable mortgages? Your escape hatch from lock-in hell. And that whispered 50-year "solution"? We'll bury it as the long-term trap it is. No more rates over 3% until we hit maximum homeownership— because a nation of renters is a nation of serfs. Let's fund the Dream with bonds, not bondage.

The Mortgage Application Gauntlet: How the Game Is Rigged (And How to Hack It)

Applying for a mortgage feels like a Soviet bread line—endless waits, arbitrary denials, and gatekeepers deciding your fate based on algorithms older than your parents. But knowledge is the hacksaw. As of 2025, the process takes 30–45 days end-to-end, with Fannie Mae's underwriting tweaks making approvals slightly easier for first-timers (e.g., more flexible DTI ratios). Here's the step-by-step takedown:

- **Pre-Approval (1–3 Days: Your Fake-Out Weapon)**: Shop lenders online and use AI. Submit basics: Income proof (W-2s, pay stubs), assets (bank statements), credit pull (aim for 620+ FICO). Get a "pre-approval letter"—it's bluff money that makes sellers take you seriously without locking in rates.

- **Formal Application (Up to 1 Week: The Interrogation)**: Once under contract, file Form 1003. Expect deep dives: Debts, employment history (2 years), gift letters for down payments. Lender runs full credit (hard inquiry—shop within 30 days to count as one).

- **Processing & Underwriting (3–7 Days + 1–3 Weeks: The Black Box)**: Docs flood in—tax returns, bank logs. Underwriters verify everything; appraisers value the home (AI-assisted now, cutting time 20%). Red flags? Income gaps or high DTI (>43%) = denial. Pro tip: Use AI tools like in Chapter 9 to preempt issues.

- **Conditional Approval & Closing (1–2 Weeks: The Finish Line)**: Clear conditions (e.g., updated pay stub). Sign at closing—bring cashier's check for down payment + costs. Rates lock 30–60 days out; shop points to buy down (1 point = 0.25% off rate, ~$2K upfront on $400K loan).

Hacks: Apply with three lenders simultaneously. Use government programs (below) for leniency. Total cost? 1–2% origination fees- slashable through negotiation. But why play their game when better options exist?

Alternatives to the Banker Trap: Land Contracts, Government Life lines, and the 2–3% Revolution Bond.

Ditch the full mortgage if it smells like servitude. Start with these escapes:

The Call to Arms: The Revolution Bond. No Rates Over 3% Until Every Dreamer Owns a Home.

Image this - you decide to move - you have AI pick out a house- you and the seller (supported by ai) agree on a price and move date - and that's it. Your belongings are shipped and you move in.

Just like TSA Precheck — Every qualified American gets a 3% mortgage from a sovereign fund or Revolution Bond - (standard underwriting criteria, collateralized by owner occupied properties in the United States of America) — administered by the federal treasury - zero closing costs. It's a simple balance sheet, tied to your IRS account. Bifurcate owner occupied mortgages from all other bonds/mortgages/influence from the Federal Reserve.

Late pays? treat them like a reverse mortgage. Just adjust the balance sheet to show decreased equity for the homeowner. At 3% interest and 3% inflation, the balance of the debt should be paid off via the increase in home value at death or departure.

AI can program that software in a couple seconds. No Wall Street no "Market Maker" needed. The market is 3%, now just fill the order.

No middleman- no real estate agent, no mortgage broker, no surveying, no banker, no bond salesperson, no investment banker, no title insurance company, no PMI company, ai underwriting, block self insured cities w/backup reinsurance - for 97% of the people that want to own vs rent.   Fannie and Freddie remain in a very subdued form and can handle the remaining 3+% based on risk. (And leave Fannie/Freddie as part of the government - only shrunk down by 95%). Taking Fannie/Freddie public sounds a little sketch.

Don't print money that causes inflation - take in investments, taxes, assessments and tariffs, investment from other countries that want to do business in America, tranche percentage requirements in investment portfolios - and then rally the nation like when we were asking for war bonds.

This is not a "hand out" it's a "hand up".   Imagine that in 30 years, everyone that wanted a home, owned one, free and clear and the money we started with was still in the bank, with interest paid to the investors?

Blockchain title and mortgage, digital arial survey with 3D building images stored in a permanent decentralized database with printed physical backup.

You don't keep an inefficient system in place - just because that's the way it's always been. Keep the old system in place - until it withers and dies— Retrain the people displaced- implement the new system now.

High rates aren't market forces—they're policy failures. At 6%*+, renting "affords" more than owning for 80% of millennials (that's a fertility killer). We demand: Sub-3% Mortgage bonds until 80+% homeownership, portable mandates, and land ownership protections. Shuffle funding to shelter, not yachts. A maxed-out homeowner nation solves crime, boosts birthrates, and ignites innovation. Renters build empires for landlords. Owners? They build America.

By funding a $15 trillion at 3% interest US government sovereign/mortgage program (the approximate current balance of Fannie/Freddie approved mortgages) it would help make homeownership universally accessible to all qualified Americans. It's mechanically possible, economically feasible and could reducing the typical $80,000 cost of buying and selling a $700,000 home to near zero. By funding this through investment requirements—not money printing— and having the program backed by the existing $80-100 trillion in U.S. property value, it's a very safe asset and represents a manageable 20% debt-to-value ratio for investors.

The economic analysis suggests this $15 trillion intervention—comparable to WWII mobilization or Social Security's creation—would save households $3,000-$6,000 annually by refinancing existing mortgages down from 6-7% down to 3%, injecting $300-$500 billion in new consumer spending. While it would increase debt-to-GDP by roughly 50%, the government would hold $15 trillion in performing mortgage assets, making the net impact far less severe than raw debt figures suggest. The critical success factors include pairing the program with aggressive housing supply expansion through zoning reform and modular construction to prevent runaway price inflation, and strictly limiting access to certified owner-occupants to avoid speculation. Done correctly, this could represent the largest middle-class wealth transfer since WWII, stabilizing shelter costs (35% of CPI), improving geographic mobility, and narrowing wealth inequality. Political discipline, insiders with heavy conflicts of interest and execution remain the decisive variables between transformative success and inflationary disaster.

- **Land Contracts (Contract for Deed): This is the smart money. Seller-Financed Freedom with Teeth.** You make payments directly to the seller (like rent- to-own, but you get equitable title immediately). Pros: Easier to qualify (no bank credit check), lower closing costs ($1K vs. $10K), flexible terms. In 2025, they're booming for rural properties and fixer-uppers—buyers build equity without an appraisal. Cons: Balloon payment at the end (e.g., a $50K lump sum after five years), risk losing all payments on default (no foreclosure protections), and the seller's mortgage could trigger acceleration if unpaid. Hack: Insist on title insurance and escrow—treat it like a mini-mortgage. Ideal for your notes' "work-for-a-house" vision.
- -**Government Financing: The People's Arsenal.**
- Many states have great programs. In Massachusetts start with Mass Housing. They have some excellent programs that help with financing and down payment, up to $25-30,000 and a low rate. https://www.MyMassHome.org
- As of November 2025, FHA (3.55% down, 580+ credit, insures up to $498K loans), VA (0% down for vets, no PMI), and USDA (0% down rural, income-capped) are processing post-shutdown hiccups. Rates? Often 0.5–1% below conventional (5.62% FHA avg). Trump's team is eyeing expansions, but we demand more: Zero-down for all essential workers.
- **The 2–3% Government-Backed Bond: Our Revolutionary Moonshot.**
- "$1T tranches backed by blockchain property," imagine Uncle Sam issuing tax-free bonds at 2–3%—directly funding homeowner loans until we hit 80% ownership (up from 65%). It's a paper shuffle: Gov prints bonds, buys/ sells to investors, funnels low-rate loans. Pros: Caps payments at renting levels ($1,500/mo. on $300K vs.$2,000 at 6%), builds equity fast, stabilizes communities. Cons? Inflation risk if overdone—but cap at "afford over rent" qualifiers. This isn't charity; it's national security. A housed nation innovates; renters revolt.

** LAND BANKS: Community "banks" or pools of funds provided by local community individuals or organizations for the sole purpose of lending to buyers for the purchase of owner occupied property in the community.

Option	**Down Payment**	**Avg Rate (Jan 2026)**	**Pros**	**Cons**	**Revolution Fit**
Traditional Mortgage	3–20%	6.12% (30-yr)	Widely available	High interest, servitude	Low—reform it
Land Contract	10–20%	5–7% (negotiated)	Flexible, no bank	Balloon risk, no title	Medium—quick entry
FHA/VA/USDA	0–3.5%	5.62%	Low barriers	PMI fees, limits	High—gov starter
2–3% Gov Bond Loan	0–5%	2–3%	Affordable Dream	Policy fight needed	Ultimate—max ownership

Portable Mortgages: Your Get-Out-of-Jail-Free Card

Rate lock-in effect? The plague where 3% rate holders sit on 40 million "golden handcuff" homes, starving inventory. Enter portable mortgages: Take your low rate *with you* when you move. Trump's admin is "actively evaluating" this, inspired by UK/ Canada models—transfer the loan to a new property, no refi needed. Pros: Keeps your 3% magic alive, boosts turnover (2.8% homes sold in 2025? Pathetic). Cons: Lender approval required, caps on value jumps. This is liberty: Move for life changes without rate rape. Demand it now—it's the antidote to stagnation.

The 50-Year Mortgage: Long-Term Servitude in Disguise Trump's floating 50-year loans to "jump-start" sales, promising lower monthly payments ($1,200 vs. $2,000 on $300K at 6%). But wake up—this is a velvet handcuff. Pros? Short-term cash flow for young families. Cons: You'd pay double the interest ($400K+ total), build equity at a snail's pace (barely own it after 20 years), and face higher rates (7%+ due to risk). It's not freedom; it's extending the plantation to your grandkids. We'd rather cap at 30 years with <3% rates—pay off faster, own sooner.

The Latest Move - Borrow from 401K for Down Payment

Stay away from this one. Find another way. Diversify, don't over leverage.

Capital Gains Deduction for the Value of the Home

Best idea of 2026. Let's see if that happens.

"Trump Homes" Rent to Own - Zero Money Down

Great idea. Rent for 3 years and then apply/credit rent payments, in some way, to the down payment. Let's see if that happens.

Red Flag - Sometimes builders "inflate" the price in order to pay points to the bank to lower the start rate of the interest rate. Make sure you are not overpaying for the property and that the "strike price" or "purchase price" is locked in up front.

Scam Alert - How is the price inflated? What you don't know, you don't know:

Once the first spec house is built - and sold — that's the most important "comparable" that a bank uses to finance a mortgage.

So - for example - a builder has 100 buildable lots. A new house sale value in the area may have been $500,000 - but this builder bumps the price up to $600,000 and offers to pays 3 points to "buy down" (lower) the initial interest rate and correspondingly the initial monthly payment costs.

The concrete company owner's sister…. that is getting the builders contract for all 100 lots, buys the house at the inflated value. Now the following appraisers use that comparable to finance all subsequent purchases.

Without due diligence, scenarios like that could pass underwriting, and fool you as a buyer. It could also be compared to money laundering in artwork and other inflated assets. Now you know.

Revolutionary Action Steps

- **Audit Your Chains**: Pull your credit today—fix errors, shop 3 lenders for pre-approval under 30 days.
- **Explore Escapes**: Run numbers on FHA/land contracts via Bankrate —aim for <4% effective rate.
- **Portable Push**: Petition your rep: "Mandate portability now!" Share #PortableMortgageRevolt.
- **Bond the Vision**: Calculate your "2–3% Dream Payment"—post it online, rally for the policy.
- **Servitude Slayer**: Swear off 50-year traps—commit to 15–30 years max, extra principal monthly.

We've mapped the minefield. Now, fund the uprising. Your home

awaits— not as a loan, but a launchpad.

Next: Contracts that don't chain you. Let's liberate the land.

Chapter 7

"Buyer's Agents Work for Free" and 5 Other Lies That Could Cost You $1,000's

The Multiple Listing Service Monopoly – How the MLS Became the New OPEC

You've scouted the turf, crunched the financials, and stared down the competition like the predator you are. But in Massachusetts, where attorneys are as mandatory as chowder on a Friday, the deal doesn't seal with a handshake—it's forged in fine print. These forms aren't just legalese; they're your shield against the sharks, your sword against the scams. Post-NAR 2025 updates from the Massachusetts Association of REALTORS® (MAR) have injected transparency steroids into every page, mandating clear commission discussions and buyer-broker agreements before you even sniff a showing. No more "free" agents or hidden splits—the Revolution demands you read, negotiate, and own every clause.

In the Bay State, the journey from listing to keys unfolds like this: The seller signs a Listing Contract, disclosing agency and commissions upfront. The buyer counters with an Offer to Purchase, backed by disclosures like lead paint. If vibes align, the Purchase & Sale Agreement locks it in, paving the way to closing. Attorneys review everything— expect $1,500–$3,000 in fees, but it's your moat against disputes. We'll break down the big five, with real-world examples pulled from MAR's 2025 library and state mandates. **These aren't templates to copy-paste; they're blueprints to customize with your lawyer.**

Pro tip: Use MAR's Remine Docs+ (free for members) for e-signing—it's the digital guillotine for paperwork delays.

Negotiate like your Dream depends on it—because it does. Sellers: Hold firm on price, dangle concessions. Buyers: Waive what you can, but never your inspection. In MA's hot 2026 market (median $650K, up 8% YoY), clarity wins; ambiguity loses deals. Let's dissect the arsenal.

1. Listing Contract (MAR Form #400: Exclusive Right to Sell Listing Agreement – Updated 2025)

This is the seller's battle cry: A binding pact granting your agent exclusive rights to market and sell, typically 3–6 months. Post-NAR, the 2025 version axes "net" commissions (no more fuzzy math on buyer agent pay) and mandates a Compensation Certification Addendum (#410), forcing explicit broker-to-broker splits. Why? To end the cartel—sellers now dictate if/how much they offer buyer agents, off-MLS.

Key Elements:

• Property details (address, legal description).

• Listing price and agent duties (marketing, showings).

• Commission: 4–6%* total, split (e.g., 2.5%* each side)—negotiable, with a checkbox for "seller offers $X to buyer broker" or "none."

• Termination clauses (e.g., 60-day notice).

• Post-NAR addendum: Arbitration for disputes, rejection space for co-op offers.

Example Snippet (From MAR #400, Section & – Compensation):

• "Broker's total compensation shall be % of the sale price or $ (flat fee). Seller authorizes Broker to offer compensation to buyer's broker of % or $, payable only if the transaction closes. Seller may amend this offer at any time."

Negotiation Hack: Demand a "protection clause" for post-expiration sales (1–6 months) at full commission—cap it at 50% to keep agents hungry.

2. Agency Disclosure (Mass.gov Real Estate Board Form – Mandatory Licensee-Consumer Relationship Disclosure)

Delivered at your first sit-down (or email pre-tour), this one-pager outs who's repping whom. MA law (MGL c. 112, §87RR½) requires it before discussing specifics, explaining seller's agent, buyer's agent, dual agency, or facilitator roles. 2025 updates add designated agency consent for intra-broker splits. Sign it, or no deal—it's your receipt that no one's pulling a dual-agency sneak.

Key Elements:

- Definitions: Seller's agent (owes loyalty to seller), buyer's agent (to buyer), dual (both, with consent).
- Consent for designated/dual: Written OK required pre-transaction.
- Warnings: Agents can't inspect or advise on lead paint/septic systems.

Example Snippet (From Mass.gov English Form, Page 1):

- "I/We acknowledge receipt of this Notice and understand that: (1) Seller's Agent represents the Seller; (2) Buyer's Agent represents the Buyer; (3) Dual Agent represents both, with limitations. For designated agency: [ ] Consent given / [ ] Not given."

Negotiation Hack: Insist on exclusive buyer's agency—no dual BS, which dilutes loyalty and brews conflicts.

3. Commission Disclosure (MAR Form #529: Brokerage Information, Escrow Deposit & Commission Worksheet – New 2025)

The post-NAR transparency bomb: This worksheet logs agent deals, escrow, and commissions before offers fly. Updated February 1, 2025, it captures buyer/seller broker information, co-op offers (accept/reject checkboxes), and arbitration options—ensuring no surprises at closing. Sellers: Use it to reject blanket co-op pay. Buyers: Verify your agent's cut.

Key Elements:

- Broker contacts and NRDS IDs.
- Commission splits (e.g., "Seller offers 2%* to buyer's broker if accepted").
- Escrow holder and deposit amount.
- Arbitration clause for fee fights.

Example Snippet (From MAR #529, Compensation Section):

• "Listing Broker Compensation: % / $ | Offered to Buyer's Broker: [ ] Yes % / $ [ ] No | Acceptance: [ ] Accepted [ ] Rejected | Arbitration: [ ] Opt-in for disputes."

Negotiation Hack: Buyers, tie your agent's fee to outcomes (e.g.,"1%* if under $400K"). Sellers, use "reject" to force direct buyer pay—save 2%.

4. Lead Paint Disclosure (Mass.gov Property Transfer Lead Paint Notification Certification)

MA's Lead Law (MGL c. 111, §197) mandates this for pre-1978 homes— 95% of inventory. Sellers disclose known hazards, provide the EPA pamphlet ("Protect Your Family from Lead"), and give buyers 10 days for testing. Sign before the Offer to Purchase; federal rules (42 USC §4852d) align it nationwide. Non-compliance? Fines up to $10K or lawsuits.

Key Elements:

• Seller statement: "Known lead paint? [ ] Yes (details) [ ]No."

• Buyer acknowledgment of 10-day inspection right.

• Signatures from all parties/agents.

Example Snippet (From Mass.gov Form):

• "Seller certifies: No knowledge of lead-based paint hazards on premises built pre-1978. Buyer acknowledges receipt of EPA pamphlet and right to inspect within 10 days of notification. Warning: Federal law prohibits lead tampering without certification."

Negotiation Hack: Buyers: Demand a $1K credit for testing/treatment. Sellers: Get a pre-inspection ($300) to disclose clean—builds trust, speeds sales.

5. Offer to Purchase (MAR Form #501: Contract to Purchase Real Estate – Updated 2025)

The buyer's opening salvo: A 2-page intent to buy, binding once accepted, with a 5–10% deposit. 2025 MAR revamp ties it to buyer-broker agreements (#714), adds post-NAR commission language, and mandates lead/ agency acknowledgments. It's not the final deal— that's the P&S—but back out without contingency exercise? Forfeit the deposit.

Key Elements:

• Price, deposit ($5K–$50K), and timeline (e.g., P&S in 10 days).

• Contingencies: Financing (21 days), inspection (10–14 days), lead paint.

• Broker intro and default terms (seller keeps deposit on buyer flake).

Example Snippet (From MAR #501, Section 1 – Terms):

• "Buyer offers $650,000 for [address]. Deposit: $32,500 held by [broker]. Contingent on: (a) Financing by [date]; (b) Satisfactory inspection(s) by [date]; (c) Lead paint certification. Buyer acknowledges agency/lead disclosures. Time is of the essence."

Negotiation Hack: Escalate smartly: "Beat competing offers by $1K up to $67SK, proof required." Sellers: Counter with "as-is" on minor defects.

Outline of the Purchase & Sale Agreement (MAR Standard Form – The Ironclad Closer)

The heavy hitter: A 10–20 page bible signed post-Offer, pre-closing (30–60 days out). It's the enforceable contract, incorporating Offer terms plus deep dives on title, closing costs, and reps. 2025 updates embed NAR compliance (e.g., compensation exhibits) and electronic delivery opts. Attorney-drafted or reviewed mandatory in MA.

High-Level Outline:

- **Parties & Property**: Names, full legal description, inclusions (e.g., appliances).
- **Purchase Price & Financing**: Breakdown (cash/loan), prorations (taxes, fuel).
- **Contingencies & Due Diligence**: Inspection (7-14-days MA norm), mortgage commitment, title search, radon/septic/lead.
- **Title & Closing**: Seller delivers clear title (policy $1K–$2K), closing date/location, deed type (quitclaim/warranty).
- **Representations & Warranties**: Seller discloses defects; buyer shows financial qualifications.
- **Commissions & Brokerage**: Exhibit A: Full splits, post-NAR concessions.
- **Defaults & Remedies**: Buyer default = deposit to seller; seller= specific performance or suit.
- **Riders/Addenda**: Lead certification, HOA estoppel, flood disclosure.
- **Signatures**: Notarized, with attorney certs.

Example Snippet (Section 7 – Closing Costs, From Standard MAR P&S):

- "Buyer pays: Loan fees, title insurance, half recording.
- Seller pays: Broker commissions per Exhibit A, transfer taxes ($2.25/$500 value), half recording. Prorations: Taxes/utilities as of closing."

Negotiation Hack: Insert "walk-away" for appraisal gaps >5%— protects buyers in overbid wars.

These forms are your Revolution roadmap—transparent, negotiable, and buyer/seller-empowering. But remember: In MA, "as-is" doesn't mean "hide defects"—caveat emptor has teeth. Always loop an attorney; DIY risks $10K+ in fixes.

Revolutionary Action Steps

- **Form Up**: Get an offer form from your attorney or agent and mock up an Offer for your dream home.
- **Disclose & Conquer**: Run a lead test ($300 kit) if pre-1978— preempt with results.
- **Negotiate Clinic**: Role-play P&S clauses with a partner: "Counter on inspection credit?"
- **Attorney Ally**: Budget $2K for review—find via MAR referral, not agent upsell.
- **Transparency Pledge**: Sign every form with a "commission cap" note —own your costs.

The paper's mightier than the pen. Wield it, and the Dream is yours. Next: Inspect like a surgeon—because unseen rot sinks ships.

Onward.

Chapter 8

House Structure – Peeling Back the Skin of Your Potential Prison (Or Palace)

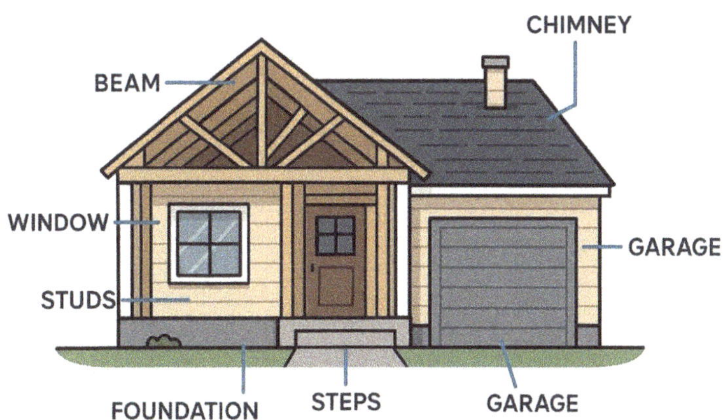

You've negotiated the forms, locked in the financing, and out-sharked the competition. But here's the revolutionary gut check: That "dream home" could be a money-socking black hole if you skip the autopsy. In Massachusetts, where 70% of the homes predate 1980 (hello, lead paint and leaky roofs), ignoring structure is like buying a Ferrari without checking the chassis—sure, it looks fast, but one pothole and you're totaled. We're not talking cosmetic fluff; we're dissecting the bones: foundations that crack like your resolve under pressure, roofs that leak secrets (and water), and systems that fail when you need them most.

The good news? The Bay State's 2025 laws just handed you a loaded scalpel. No longer can sellers or agents bully you into waiving inspections to "win" the bid—thanks to the Affordable Homes Act's ironclad protections. This isn't nanny-state meddling; it's your Bill of Rights in action, ensuring you inspect without fear of deal-killing retaliation. In this chapter, we'll map the structural battlefield, spotlight the new laws arming you against waivers, and tackle the top defects that doom deals (with fixes to turn lemons into equity). Because in the Revolution, you don't just buy a house—you buy freedom from future floods, fires, and five-figure fixes. Let's cut deep.

The Anatomy of a Home: Structural Basics Every Rebel Must Master

Homes aren't magic boxes; they're engineered beasts fighting gravity, weather, and time. In MA's freeze-thaw hell (200+ cycles yearly), structures age like fine wine—if maintained—or vinegar if ignored. Know these systems cold; they're your first line against the "unknown unknowns."

- **Foundation**: The bedrock (pun intended). MA homes are slab, crawlspace, or full basement (most common, 60% per 2025 Census data). Cracks? Normal if hairline (settling); red flags if stair-step or horizontal (shifting soil, $10K–$50K fix).
- **Framing & Walls**: Load-bearing skeleton of wood/steel studs. Inspect for rot (water intrusion), bowing (settlement), or pests (termites in old colonials). MA's seismic zone? Low, but wind loads demand solid sheathing.
- **Roof & Exterior**: Asphalt shingles rule (lifespan 20–30 years); inspect for curling, bald spots, or poor flashing around chimneys. Siding (vinyl/ clapboard) hides rot—tap for hollow sounds.
- **Windows/Doors & Envelope**: Seals against air/moisture. Energy loss here spikes bills 20–30% (DOE stats). Check seals, drafts, and egress (MA mandates two bedroom exits).
- **Mechanicals (HVAC, Plumbing, Electrical)**: The veins. HVAC: Oil/ gas furnaces common (check efficiency >80% AFUE). Plumbing: Galvanized pipes corrode; copper/PVC better. Electrical: Knob-and-tube in pre-1950s homes? Fire hazard—upgrade to 200-amp panels.

Pro tip: Hire a certified inspector (ASHI/InterNACHI, $500–$800 in MA). Add specialists for radon (30% homes elevated) or septic (rural musts).

The 2025 MA Inspection Revolution: No More Waiver Warfare

Sellers and agents used to weaponize hot markets: "Waive inspection or lose to the cash buyer!" Not anymore. The Affordable Homes Act (signed June 2025, effective October 15) slammed the door on that BS, prohibiting any sale conditioned on skipping inspections or favoring waiver offers. It's a direct shot at equity—protecting first-timers from predatory pressure in a state where median prices hit $650K.

Key Changes:
- **Mandatory Disclosure**: Sellers/REALTORS® must provide a signed "Home Inspection Rights" form before any offer, outlining your right to inspect (no penalties for exercising it). MAR updated P&S forms to embed this—non-compliance? Fines up to $5,000 or deal voiding.
- **Waiver Ban**: Can't reject offers solely for requesting inspections; must treat all equally. Buyers get 10–14 days post-Offer to inspect (standard contingency).
- **Enforcement Teeth**: AG's office oversees complaints; Realtors face license risks. Early 2025 data? Waiver rates dropped 90% in competitive markets like Greater Boston.

This law levels the arena: Sellers can't hide horrors; buyers can't be gas-lit into blindness. But it amps urgency—inspect fast, negotiate fiercely.

Common Inspection Nightmares: Spot 'Em, Fix 'Em, or Flee

MA's old homes (average age 50+ years) breed beasts. From 2025 inspection reports (ASHI aggregates), 65% flag issues; 20% kill deals. Here's the hit list, with resolutions to reclaim your power:

| **Problem** | **Why It's a Beast (MA-Specific)** | **Red Flags** | **Resolution Tactics** | **Cost Range** |.

| **Foundation Cracks** | Freeze-thaw cycles widen hairlines into chasms; common in basements (40% of flags). | Horizontal/stair-step cracks >1/4", uneven floors, water seepage. | Negotiate $5K–$20K credit for piers/epoxy injection; engineer report ($500) for leverage. Walk if structural shift. | $2K–$50K |.

Roof Leaks/Wear | Harsh winters shred shingles; poor drainage floods attics (top issue, 25% reports). | Missing granules, sagging, interior stains. | Seller replaces ($10K asphalt) or buyer credits post-inspection. Test with hose. |$5K–$15K|.

Electrical Deficiencies | Knob-and-tube in colonials sparks fires; over loads in additions (15% flags).

Chapter 9

Your AI Arsenal – 20 Battle-Tested Prompts to Crush the Real Estate Game in 2026

You now possess every weapon in the Revolution except one: the ultimate force multiplier—artificial intelligence.

These aren't fluffy ChatGPT one-liners. These are the exact prompts I (and thousands of rebels) can use daily to possibly save tens of thousands of dollars, out-negotiate agents, spot hidden defects, and close faster than the old system ever allowed.

Copy-paste them into Grok, Claude, Gemini, or Perplexity—watch the magic happen.

Pricing & Valuation (Prompts 1–4)

Instant Comps Destroyer

"Act as a Massachusetts-licensed appraiser. Using only public records and MLS data available as of November 2025, give me the 10 most recent and most similar sold comps for [exact address]. Include the sale date, sale price, beds/baths/sq.ft./lot size, condition notes, and exact adjustments (+/− per sq.ft./per bed, etc.). Provide the final estimated value range in bold."

Future Value Forecaster

"Using 2025–2030 migration trends, interest-rate forecasts, school redistricting plans, and planned infrastructure for [town/city], predict the most likely 5-year and 10-year price appreciation for a [year built] [beds/baths] home on [street]. Give three scenarios: base, bullish, bearish."

Pricing to Create a Bidding War

"In the current [town] market (inventory X months, median DOM Y days), recommend the exact list price for a [beds/baths, condition] home worth approximately \$Z that will generate multiple offers in under 10 days while maximizing final sale price. Explain your math."

Rent-vs-Buy Nuclear Calculator

"Compare buying a \$650,000 home at 6.1%* 30-yr vs renting a comparable property at \$3,200/month in [town]. Factor in 2025 MA property tax rates, insurance, HOA, maintenance, appreciation (3%/yr), rent increases (3%/yr), and tax benefits. Tell me the exact breakeven year and which is smarter for a 7-year hold."

Negotiation & Offer Writing (Prompts 5–9)

Bulletproof Offer Script (Hot Market)

"Write a full Massachusetts Offer to Purchase (MAR Form 501 language) for \$[amount] on [address] that includes an escalation clause beating any bonified offer by \$2,000 up to \$[cap], a 12-day inspection contingency, appraisal gap coverage up to \$25,000, and a seller concession of 2% toward buyer closing costs. Make it clean and aggressive."

Counter-Offer Annihilator

"The seller countered my \$675k offer at \$710k with no concessions. Write a sharp, professional response accepting \$698k, asking for \$12k in repairs/ closing credit, 60-day close, and possession 30 days post-closing (rent-back at \$0). Tone: polite but immovable."

Commission Slayer Script

"Draft a buyer-broker agreement addendum capping my agent's fee at 1.5% total (paid only at closing) and reducing it to 1% if the purchase price is under \$650k. Include performance bonuses and a termination-for-convenience clause."

Inspection Negotiation Nuke

"I just received a 42-page inspection report with \$28,000 in recommended repairs. Prioritize into must-fix, nice-to-have, and cosmetic. Draft a repair request asking the seller to fix only the top 8 items (total~\$14k) OR give a \$18k credit at closing. Attach exact report page references."

Appraisal Gap Coverage Clause

"Write a rock-solid appraisal contingency addendum for Massachusetts that says I will cover any gap up to $40,000 in non-refundable additional deposit while preserving my right to terminate and get my original deposit back if the gap exceeds $40k."

Due Diligence & Red Flags (Prompts 10–15)

Neighbor From Hell Detector

"Search public records for [exact address + next 5 surrounding parcels]. Tell me any history of police calls, code violations, registered sex offenders, tax liens, hoarding complaints, or ongoing lawsuits in the past 10 years."

Flood & Climate Risk Deep Dive

"For [address], pull the latest FEMA flood zone, First Street Foundation risk score, sea-level rise projections to 2050, wildfire risk, and whether the property is in a MA-designated Environmental Justice zone. Give me a 1– 10 danger score."

Title Issue Bloodhound

"Review the last deed and any recorded documents for [address]. Flag any clouds on title, easements, rights-of-way, party wall agreements, or pending betterment assessments that could affect value or use."

School & Redistricting Expert

"What elementary, middle, and high school is [address] assigned to in 2025–2026? Are there any approved or proposed redistricting plans that would change this by 2027? Include GreatSchools ratings and recent test-score trends."

Septic & Sewer Money Pit Checker

"Is [address] on town sewer or private septic? If septic, when was the last Title 5 inspection and result? Are there any failed systems or pending sewer betterments within 1 mile that could trigger a $25k+ assessment?"

Hidden Cost Calculator

"For a 1980s colonial in [town], estimate annual costs most buyers forget: oil heat conversion to heat pump, lead paint removal costs, asbestos removal, knob-and-tube rewiring, and MA smoke/CO detector upgrades. Total first-5-year surprise budget."

Marketing & Listing (Prompts 16–20)

Zillow-Topping Listing Description

"Write a 350-word MLS description for [address] that ranks #1 for SEO using 2025 buyer search terms. Highlight walkability, WFH office potential, robot-lawn-mower-friendly yard, and proximity to driverless-car hubs."

Coming-Soon Teaser Campaign

"Create a 7-day pre-launch social media campaign (4 posts + 3 stories) for a $749k listing in [town] that creates FOMO without violating MLS rules."

Professional Photo Shot List

"Give me the exact 42 photos (including drone, twilight, and 3D tour stills) a photographer must take of a &-bed colonial to maximize offers in Massachusetts in 2025."

Open House Script for Maximum Offers

"Write a 60-second elevator pitch + conversation starters an agent should use at an open house to turn visitors into written offers the same weekend."

Flat-Fee Listing Masterpiece

"Draft a complete flat-fee listing agreement ($5,000 total) that includes professional photos, MLS syndication, yard sign, lockbox, and offer management—but NO buyer-agent co-op unless I specifically approve it in writing."

Bookmark this chapter.

These 20 prompts alone may have saved some clients thousands of dollars per transaction in 2025.

Use them ruthlessly. Share them freely.

This is how we win the Revolution—one AI-powered deal at a time.

Next: Future cities where land serves life, not lords. The Revolution marches on.

Keep fighting.

Chapter 10

Sustainable Cities – The Vision

Throughout history, we've discussed the ideal community.

Be it The Gardens of Babylon, (as questionably noted in Fertile Crescent and ancient Greek history),

or the city of Elysium (as noted in Homer's "Odyssey" from Greek mythology), or Broadacre City as detailed by Frank Lloyd Wright,

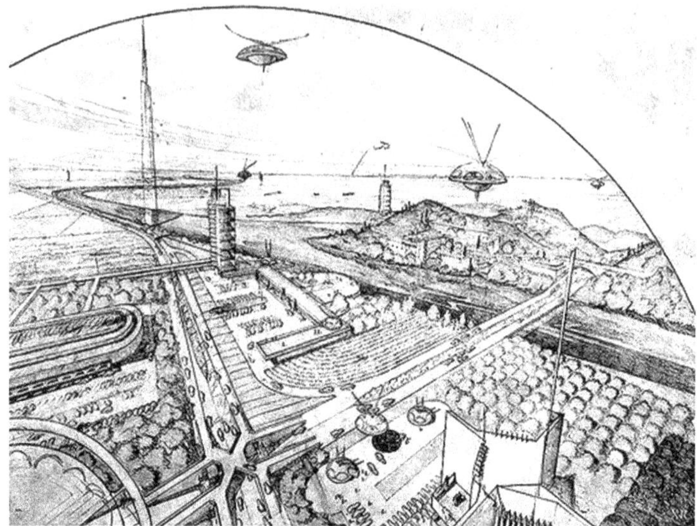

and now what we call "Sustainable Cities" — all dreamed of a better - perhaps sustainable community but no country has ever accomplished the pride of having these dreams fully realized.

Today that dream can be a reality. We can do this if we have the will and organization to do it.

Where Land Serves Life, Not Profit.

We've torn down the cartel. We've armed you to buy or sell on your terms.

Now we finish the Revolution by building the cities that make the old system obsolete.

These are not utopian sketches. They are the logical, low-cost, self-sustaining cities we can start breaking ground on tomorrow using 2025 technology, Depression-era work ethic, and the same sovereign land principles carved into the Declaration and Constitution.

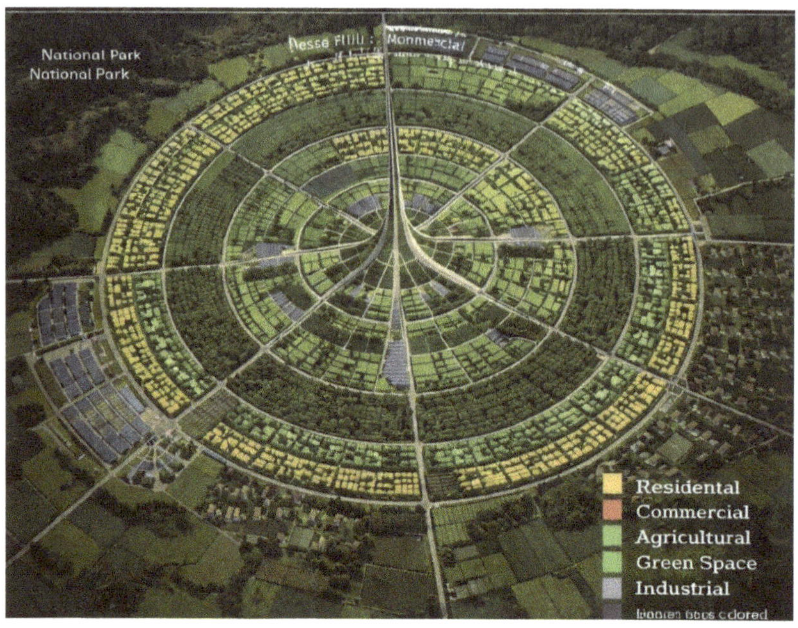

We call them Sustainable Cities. Land for the people, by the people, with out debt-slavery. Seeds of Life, pockets of renewal that will fuel others like it.

The Core Principles – Your Checklist for the New American Sustainable City — and How we can work together to make it happen:

Establish Needs - which include:

Clean Air.

Clean Water.

Nutritious Food.

Clean, Thermoregulated Shelter.

Clothing.

Electricity.

Safety and Human Belonging.

The Ability to Maintain a Healthy Body.

Access to the Pursuit of Happiness, Love, Intimacy & Social Connection.

ACTION REQUIRED:

****NATIONWIDE CONTEST TO KICK OFF the 250th ANNIVERSARY of AMERICA****

Contest to Build the BEST Sustainable City.

Quasi Public/Private partnership, coordinated by the Army Core of Engineers, alongside local builders, and compliant with equal housing standards.

Public/Private Sponsorships, "Revolution Bonds" or pledged gifts in the $4-6B range could fund an entire project.

Each state chooses it's own Champion building plan. Ideally coordinated by the local counties and with the use of state approved contractors. American competition at it's finest.

Presold Units are offered for the size of the Pre-Planed Sustainable City. 10,000 to 100,000 Pledges per state gets the ball rolling. Establish diverse guidelines for admitting citizens, based on the needs of the community, lottery, first come first serve, or whatever criteria has been agreed upon.

A community of people from all walks of life. Plumbers, carpenters, robot engineers, doctors, nurses, farmers, teachers, back hoe operators, steam fitters, electricians, stay at home parents, military personnel. Veterans, families, the handicapped, uneducated and the brilliant from all walks of life. Big, small, thin and fat. Please consider them all.

Building new is quicker and more efficient than trying to convince an old existing city to change. We need competition to force change — and the competition should embrace it, because the experience gained from Sustainable Cities benefits everyone.

According to Wallethub's (https://wallethub.com/) 2025 rankings of the greenest cities in the US, they noted:

- San Jose, CA
- Washington, DC
- Oakland, CA
- Irvine, CA
- San Francisco, CA

Globally ranked (https://www.arcadis.com/en/insights/perspectives/global/sustainable-cities-index-2024)

- Amsterdam, Netherlands
- Rotterdam, Denmark
- Copenhagen, Denmark
- Munich, Germany

If that's the bar — by starting over from scratch, we can do better. Many projects will be over budget. Some won't. Some will use a team effort to excel like no others. Corporate sponsors will come to the table with great resources and be willing to "inspire the team effort," or they won't.

The beauty of these projects will be that the financials are online and transparent. This is where science meets art. Let the games begin! Carry the torch in your community— put together your team - your plan— your bid. We have a choice today; to do nothing, to talk or to act.

The goal here is partial self-sufficiency, aiming for 50–80% of food needs met on-site (prioritizing fresh produce, greens, fruits, eggs, and some proteins via vertical/aquaponic systems and perimeter polyculture farms). The remaining 20–50% comes from regional trade networks—grains, oils, specialty items—keeping the community resilient but connected.

- With vertical farming: Yields 10–100x higher per land area, slashing needs dramatically (e.g., leafy greens/hydroponics use 90–99% less land/water).

For Sustainable City's radial, biophilic design (central Spire + perimeter homes + vast green surface), we optimize with:

- Vertical farms in the Spire (multi-story hydro/aero/aquaponics for greens, herbs, fruits).
- Perimeter polyculture (permaculture orchards, community gardens, small livestock).
- Green roofs/terraces everywhere. Recommended Targets for Sustainable Cities Ideal Population: 10,000–150,000 residents.
- Why this range?
- Small enough for strong community cohesion, minimal services (robotic education/AI security vision works best here—predictive systems scale efficiently up to ~20k).
- Large enough for economic viability (shared amenities, vertical farms, SMR/solar infrastructure) and diverse housing (Spire condos+ perimeter single-family).
- For comparison, the Burj Khalifa in Dubai has about 1,000 residential units, 163 floors, and can accommodate 10,000 people. It's mix of residential, commercial and hospitality spaces make it a unique comparison for our Sustainable City model. It cost $1.5 billion to build and took 5 years to build. The project employed over 12,000 workers and 22 million man-hour total.

Total Land Expanse: 5,000–10,000 acres (10 sq mi / 25 sq km) (Add extra points if you Sustainable City abuts a conservancy.) The average county in the US contains around 400,000 acres. Keep in mind, existing land owners/farmers can retain their ownership. It's the contracted rules that matter. It's a trade off, both good and bad. There just needs to be a "meeting of the minds" as to who has what specific rights.

Breakdown for ~70–80% food self-sufficiency:

- Built/dense zones (Spire + inner housing): 300–600 acres (high-rise/terraced, minimal land for living).
- Green surface/parks/forests/buffers: 1,000–3,500 acres (biophilic wellness, recreation, wildlife corridors).
- Dedicated food production: 600–1,200 acres (~0.05–0.1 acres/ person gross, but effective 0.2–0.5 with vertical stacking).
- 200–400 acres horizontal (perimeter permaculture, orchards, pasture for eggs/poultry/small dairy).
- Equivalent of 400–800 acres in vertical (Spire-integrated farms: 10–20x yield boost).
- This yields:
- Density: Overall ~3,000–5,000 people/sq mi (sustainable mid- range; Vancouver ~5,400 is highly livable).
- Food output: Covers most perishables locally (ultra-fresh, zero-mile), imports dry goods/proteins for resilience/diversity.

• Benefits: Vast surface greenery (70%+ non-built), subterranean utilities preserve ecology, atomic/solar powers controlled environments year-round.

Quick Food & Diet Breakdown

For partial self-sufficiency (70–80% on-site, import grains/meat/ oils):

• Diet assumption: American mixed (omnivore-leaning, ~2,500 kcal/ day/person), shifting toward plant-heavy for efficiency.

• Regional crops (assume Midwest/Southwest adaptable site for versatility):

• Vertical (Spire-integrated hydro/aquaponics): Leafy greens, herbs, tomatoes, berries, strawberries—high-yield, year-round (10–30x traditional).

• Perimeter polyculture/permaculture: Orchards (apples, nuts), root veggies (potatoes, carrots), legumes, corn, small livestock (eggs, poultry, limited dairy).

• Output: ~600–1,200 acres dedicated (incl. vertical equivalent) covers most fresh produce/fruits/proteins; import wheat/rice/exotics.

• Benefits: Ultra-fresh, low transport emissions; community gardens boost engagement.

Housing Numbers

• Average household size: ~2.5 persons (2025 U.S. avg.).

• Total households: ~4,800 (for 12,000 residents).

• Mix: 40% Spire condos (higher density, urban vibe), 60% perimeter single-family (privacy/American preference) ~1,920 condos,~2,880 SFHs.

Central Spire Enhancements

• Includes: Robotic/AI medical facilities (telemedicine, autonomous diagnostics/surgery bots, preventive care)—handling 80–90% routine/urgent needs; minimal human staff.

• Fire-proofing: All structures use non-combustible materials (steel/ CLT with fire-retardant treatments), full sprinklers, smart sensors with near-zero fire risk, minimal fire/police (AI drones, community response).

Cost Breakdown (2026 Estimates)

Assumptions (conservative # of units, sustainable/net-zero premium ~5–10% extra for efficiency/solar):

• Condo unit: Avg. 1,000 sq ft.

• Cost: $700/sq ft (high-rise multifamily, sustainable) ~$700,000/unit.

• SFH: Avg. 2,400 sq ft net-zero.

• Cost: $200–300/sq ft (incl. premium) ~$600,000/home.

• Total residential: ~$3-4 billion (excl. infrastructure/energy/farms ~$1–2B more; grand total ~$4–6B for community).

Development Cost Analysis

Residential Units

Type	# Units	@ (sq. ft)	$/sq ft	Unit $	Total
Spire Condos	1,920	1,000 sq ft	$700	$700K	$1.34B
SFH's	2,880	2,400 sq ft	$250	$600K	$1.73B
Total	**4,800**				**$3.07B**

Infrastructure

Subterranean roads/utilities, parks, small modular reactor (SMR)/solar, vertical farms: **$1.5B**

Total Buildout

$4-6B

Financing & Labor Model

Donated Private Funds — People like to solve problems. Consider corporate sponsors like Binghatti City in Dubai, the 10 million square foot building sponsored by Mercedes Benz. Better yet, Imagine having a contest in all 50 states for the best design and implementation. **50 States — $5B Bond@ — $250B Total Spend**

Yes — Costs very well may be higher - but this gives perspective.

For Comparison:

Cost of one aircraft carrier: USS Gerald R Ford: $13B Cost of one B-2 Aircraft: $2B.

Cost of one Columbia-Class submarine: $16B (we just ordered a dozen).

Savings from changing MA sales tax from 5% to 4% = $4.2B savings/ year.

US military budget for 2026: $1.1 trillion++.

Microsoft and Meta spending on data centers: @ $80 Billion each Where are our priorities? and who's needs are we taking care of?

The beauty of this concept is that only a couple of people need to fund it to make it happen. We're lucky to have a president who can approve the development with the stroke of a pen. Trump knows how real estate works. Approving large building projects is easy for him. Imagine the cost savings with minimal sunk costs in design and holding.

Other Candidates:

Nicole Shanahan (and ex Sergey Brin) — They have the funds ($140 Billion net worth) Nicole is very knowledgeable in the Sustainable City field.

Alice Walton $106B Julia Koch $81B Jacqueline Mars $42B Miriam Adelson $37B Abigail Johnson $35B.

Billionaire philanthropist MacKenzie Scott donated $7.17B in 2025 or any corporate, public or governmental foundation willing to stand up and make a difference in every state in America.

• Buildout funding: Government grants (infrastructure/sustainability incentives), investors (long-term returns via low operating costs - run by AI).

• Resident equity: Humans contribute 4–5 years labor (construction/maintenance, robotic-assisted for efficiency) "sweat equity" offsets unit cost (e.g., earn ~$100–200k credit toward home/condo).

• Attraction: Zero property tax (community-funded via energy ex ports/farms), ultra-low utilities (net-zero + atomic/solar), affordable effective ownership and draws families seeking stability/wellness. This creates equitable access while bootstrapping the build. Later phases incorporate robotics for speed/cost reduction.

** Financial Freedom -Low interest or near-zero mortgages**

The United Service Organization (USO) 2.0 – led by the Army Corps of Engineers versus a developer. Local labor and civilian construction force, augmented by major construction companies. Bigger than the Marshall Plan (total cost $13.3B in 1948 - $137B in 2024 dollars) only this time it's rebuilding America.

Estimated cost to rebuild Ukraine: $524B.

New plan to rebuild Gaza? $70B and it will be done in four years. Amazingly conceived and under construction in less than an month, while Memphis and South Chicago have been failing for decades and no reconstruction project is even considered.

America used to have the best cities in the world. We need to see action on "America First". If there's a will in America — there is a way.

Any able-bodied citizen aged 18 and up can "volunteer" for five years. You learn a trade, live in barracks, eat well, and bank equity instead of rent.

At the end of your term you are deeded – with a small mortgage or free and clear – one of the homes your crew built.

No interest. No PMI. No banker. Just sweat equity and pride of ownership.

Veterans, builders and essential workers jump the line.

Vertical density surrounded by horizontal freedom

Central clusters of elegant 100–200-story spires and terraces (think Frank Lloyd Wright's Broadacre City meets the Price Tower on steroids).

Every resident lives within 15 minutes of open land, but the population density is concentrated so 80–90% of the footprint remains green.

Massive greenspace and greenhouses with integrated livestock and wildlife.

Between the spires: rolling pastures, orchards, and community gardens. Local greenhouses cover most of food needs.

Cattle, sheep, goats, and chickens graze in rotating paddocks right in the city.

Children learn animal husbandry the way previous generations learned to ride bikes.

Manure feeds methane digesters and compost. Zero food miles for dairy, eggs, and beef.

Solar Panels
Vaccume Tubes
Electric Roadway
Utilities & Electrical

All major traffic underground

Personal cars park in centralized garages on the outer ring.

Inside the city: silent electric carts and golf-cart-style pods run in climate-controlled subterranean tunnels topped with solar canopies.

Surface roads are for walking, biking, horses, and the occasional emergency vehicle.

Wildlife corridors cross freely above ground – no more roadkill and segregation of wildlife habitats.

Every obstruction buried

Power, fiber, water, sewer, mail tubes, trash/recycling pneumatic tubes – everything underground.

No poles, no wires, no mailboxes, no signs cluttering the horizon. The skyline is spires, trees, and sky.

Solar everywhere that doesn't breathe

Solar film on every spire balcony, every tunnel roof, every parking canopy. Transparent Luminescent Solar Concentrators (TLSC's) that capture UV/IR solar energy and let visible light thru to grow plants, as well as Perovskite panels on south-facing terraces.

Small modular reactors or geothermal as backup – the city exports power to the old grid and earns revenue.

Local greenhouses and vertical farms inside the towers Lower 20 floors of each spire dedicated to hydroponics, mushrooms, and aquaponics. Residents "shop" by walking downstairs with a basket.

One-acre homestead option

For those who complete a second five-year tour or who qualify through other service, you can opt for a full Broadacre-style one-acre plot with a Usonian-inspired Wright house on the outer greenbelt – still mortgage- free.

Governance by ownership

Only residents vote on city matters (town hall, one vote per citizen over the age of 18). Here's the thing — since the "condo" rules were outlined from start, there should be very little need to enact new rules or laws. Two-thirds+ majority rule to change laws.

Renting is allowed but rare and temporary – the economic engine is designed to turn every renter into an owner within a decade.

Built to last 500 years, maintained for free

USO crews never disband – after the city is built they become the perpetual maintenance and expansion force.

No property-tax funded bureaucracy; a small condo fee and energy-export surcharges keeps everything running.

The Numbers (2025 dollars)

- Cost to house one builder/participant for five years (barracks, food, training, tools): ~$180,000.
- Value of the home they receive minus work credits at the end: $550,000–$800,000.
- Net mortgage debt to the Revolution Bond per new homeowner: under $420,000 after energy sales and material efficiencies.
- Compare to current system: $700,000 in mortgage costs, plus $400,000+ in interest over 30 years to a bank.

The Visual (Close your eyes and see it)

Dawn. You walk out onto a 147th-floor terrace wrapped in ivy. Below, spirals of white spires rise from a sea of green. Cattle graze between the towers. A trophy deer crosses the old surface road that is now a bike path and once near extinct species thrive. Silent pods glide beneath your feet on their way to the maglev ring that shoots riders to Boston or Providence in twelve minutes. The air smells of fresh bread from the tower bakery and clover from the pasture. No sirens. No horns. No rent check.

This is not science fiction. This is what happens when we decide debt-free land and honest work are once again the American birthright.

Revolutionary Action Steps – Start Tomorrow

- Contact Funding sources and get their pledge. Ask your Congressman and Senator: Demand pilot funding for the first 10-50,000-person Sustainable Cities on targeted areas that have an acceptable location. Consider federal land for even quicker implementation (we have millions of acres doing nothing). America has a coordination and distribution problem, as much as it has a population problem.
- Form your local "Sustainable City Chapter Group" – 100 people willing to be the first volunteer cohort.
- Share this chapter with the hashtag #RealEstateRevolution" – make it impossible to ignore. Visit https://www.realestaterevolution.org/ for more information.

The old cities were built to extract. These cities will be built to liberate. The Revolution is no longer about beating the system.

It's about replacing it with something worthy of the Declaration you can read below.

Onward to the first groundbreaking. The dirt is waiting.

And this time, it belongs to us. To quote our Founders:

"**When in the Course of human events, it becomes necessary for one people to dissolve the political bands which have connected them with another, and to assume among the powers of the earth, the separate and equal station to which the Laws of Nature and of Nature's God entitle them, a decent respect to the opinions of mankind requires that they should declare the causes which impel them to the separation.**

We hold these truths to be self-evident, that all men are created equal, that they are endowed by their Creator with certain inalienable Rights, that among these are **Life, Liberty and the pursuit of Happiness"

FIRST PRINCIPALS on Land Ownership

Let's face it: we can't create new, peaceful communities unless we change what we've done in the past. "King/Queen of the Hill" and "Survival of the Fittest" only go so far.

With full recognition of some elemental basic human rights (such as the right to live in peace, and that no one can take another person's land or property by force), we can build new communities on solid footings.

Since time began, politics and real estate have been intermingled. In times of war or personal conflict—when it comes down to the end and you boil it down—what it's usually about is who "controls" the land and the people who live there.

Those who "control" the land - have taxing powers. In America - those powers are given to the leaders - by the voters. That's unique in history of the world.

You have the power to better your rights. Just do it.

Siting USO/Sustainable City Communities

**Land Considerations **

Location: Rural contiguous areas within a short distance to major roads. This way much of the sunk costs are offset by existing infrastructure. Local/County buy-in needed.

Population: Run the numbers for the different sized communities. Consider a minimum of 10,000 people and a maximum of 300,000 people per community.   There's no right answer and will depend upon the total package and location.

Water: Sufficient to cover the needs of the community without having adverse impacts on the water table or water supply.

Sewer: Sewage treatment on site to handle all waste water and garbage disposal. Toxic chemicals are screened coming in and removed before disposal.

Power: Fully sustainable solar with atomic or fossil fuel backup system. Communication Systems: Phone/computer/robotics all via satellite or other wireless networks.

Roads: Subterranean made for electric vehicles or mass transport wherever possible to maximize green space.

Food: Greenhouses disbursed through the community and professionally managed allows for fresh food and produce year round. Common areas allow for socialization and community involvement.

Wildlife: Designated habitats for wildlife and domestic food production.

First Principles of Taxation

Start at zero and breakdown what is absolutely necessary for the community to combine funds in order to achieve economies of scale.

For example: Property taxes - Current National Average:

K-12 Public Schools 45-50% of budget.

City/ Municipal 20-25% (Police, fire, streets, parks, libraries, admin).

County 15-20% Sheriff, jails, courts, health dept., roads.

Community College 4-4% Higher Education.

Special Districts 5-10% Water, sewer, fire protection, hospitals, mosquito control, etc.

Cut Real Estate Taxes By Doing The Following

The few condos that are available for rent at the Spire are controlled by the condominium association through the board.

Commercial units at the Spire are leased and controlled by the condominium association itself.

The Sustainable City is self-insured, covering all units within the community. Condo fees cover selected services.

Base electrical service is covered.

There is little risk of fire due to concrete construction and integrated fire-suppression systems within the building.

Video surveillance in public areas and robotic policing limit risk to human life and help ensure safety and equal justice under the law.

Robotic supervision of offenders could be implemented to reduce detention and incarceration costs.

Robotically controlled hospitals will help streamline healthcare delivery.

No drone zone over property as deliveries can all be taken to a perimeter warehouse and delivered to your door subterranean. No UPS trucks, no daily mail truck delivery necessary beyond the exterior boundary.

We need a healthy community—everyone in a sustainable community should have access to the healthcare they need.

Cost savings from housing, insurance, transportation, and taxes will help offset healthcare costs.

Healthier meals provided by local farms and prepared by local restaurants will also contribute to better health.

Bottom Line

IF education is handled by your desired algorithm and robotic instructors provide personalized unlimited education for free, why stick with a current system?

Please don't get me wrong. I honor and respect our current teachers and educational system, law enforcement, and fire fighters. Same for real estate agents, insurance agents and mortgage originators. You've gotten us to where we are today. The best in the world.

But Back to the Bottom Line - Change is Here

With personalized robotic education, K-Higher Education can be removed from the budget. That does not mean we don't need human teachers.   We just need a different structure.

That's a 50-60% savings in real estate taxes- right off the top. With Pex/flexible plastic tubing, fire suppression systems in single family residential becomes a great option over that of traditional expensive firetruck, fireman, firehouse type systems.

Cut Police and Fire by 90% - robotic police officers are safer and don't require a public pension. Imagine that - number of pensions reduced by 90%.   Forever.

That's another 20-40% savings

Library? Maybe we call them central gathering centers— while this one might be an easy place to cut - Let's "repurpose " the space for community events.

5% - added back - collected in monthly condo fee - or could be paid for on a per use charge- then we'd zero it out.

What's that leave?

Administrative?

Ok - let's put in that 5% cost again.

AI can help manage budgets — big decisions could be resolved "on line" with community involvement. It would not be hard to zero this one out as well — but someone has to do it…

Judges and prosecutors:

That leaves 5% for the criminal justice system, the attorneys, the judges, and the courts.

Unless we utilized AI, and make the people that used the courts, pay for the costs? (Instead of the innocent people paying).

Consider zeroing this out and combining with the "Administrative Budget".

Subterranean Roads :

Much easier to maintain- especially in winter or harsh weather conditions. Lightweight transportation easier on roads- no heavy snowplows or semi trucks allowed. Goods and services delivered via lightweight mass transportation tunnels and routed to individual units via built in vacuum tubes.

Tolls can cover costs vs. taxes Zero out cost for roads

Water:

Water is free from the earth, pumping it is not that expensive at a centralized spire. Distribution systems and maintenance are greatly reduced because most everything is centralized.

Sewer :

This cost likely remains. Let's call it 3-5% of the total budget. While this is automated, there's a cost to clean up, and it needs to be done right in order to maintain a healthy and sustainable environment.

The Final Question

We can do better. This isn't rocket science. Humans have built many homes and communities throughout time - but none seem to be very sustainable. We have a moment in time where we can change that.

If by creating efficiencies in our cities, we lowered the costs for housing, insurance , and tax costs (as we previously discussed) to less than 10% of our income, would that be helpful to the overall economy?

How much further down the path of non-sustainability must we charge before it's gone forever? If we created new sustainable communities that the entire world could learn from, would that be helpful to the world?

Can borders and lot lines be digitized and honored?

So now you know what you know, and you will never unknow.

Will you take action? https://www.realestaterevolution.org/

Join us today.

Chapter 11

The Sacred Texts of Freedom – The Declaration, Constitution, Bill of Rights, and the Bloody History of Who Owns the Dirt

We hold this truth to be self-evident: In America, the fight for homeownership isn't just about bricks and mortar— it's about blood, soil, and the unyielding grip on land that has defined our nation's soul since the first musket cracked at Lexington. Property rights aren't a footnote in the founding documents; they're the goddamn foundation. The Declaration of Independence didn't just declare war on tea taxes—it proclaimed that life, liberty, and the pursuit of happiness (read: property, per John Locke) were God-given, not king-granted. The Constitution wired the circuits to protect your plot from government greed. The Bill of Rights slammed the door on seizures without a fair shake.

But here's the revolutionary gut punch: These words were inked in the shadow of conquest. The "first Americans" (Pilgrims, that is) didn't homestead empty fields—they seized them from Native tribes in Plymouth, MA, under the hypocritical banner of "discovery," turning sacred grounds into auction blocks. We can only imagine how Massasoit was conflicted as he helped the Pilgrims survive the first winter.

Fast-forward to 2025/26, and echoes ring in modern power plays, like Donald Trump's blunt-force Gaza gambit: "We're going to take it," he said, dangling U.S. control as the ultimate negotiation hammer—like yanking a toy from two squabbling kids until they play nice. Or a Venezuela grab-and-go or the Greenland, "ask for everything but take what you need". If you can be nice, great—I'll hand it back. If not? Nobody wins the dirt.

Brilliant? Brutal? Both. It mirrors America's founding land heists— take control, redistribute on *your* terms. But in real estate? Weaponize it: Facing a stalled multi-offer? "Walk away—I'll let the next buyer have it, or we split concessions." History teaches: He who controls the dirt dictates the peace.

Why study this history? Because ignoring it dooms us to repeat it: gatekept dreams, inflated commissions, zoning wars that price out the tribe. We've been lied to long enough. These documents aren't dusty relics—they're your Declaration of Real Estate Independence. Study them. Weaponize them. Then, join us in forging the Real Estate Revolution of Real Estate Rights, where property isn't plunder, but power for all.

Below, we reprint key excerpts from the sacred trio (sourced from the National Archives, 2025 editions). We've outlined property tied passages for your revolutionary eyes. Read. Reflect. Revolt.

In CONGRESS, July 4, 1776.

The unanimous Declaration of the thirteen united States of America.

When in the Course of human events, it becomes necessary for one people to dissolve the political bands which have connected them with another, and to assume among the Powers of the earth, the separate and equal station to which the Laws of Nature and of Nature's God entitle them, a decent respect to the opinions of mankind requires that they should declare the causes which impel them to the separation.

We hold these truths to be self-evident, that all men are created equal, that they are endowed by their Creator with certain unalienable Rights, that among these are Life, Liberty and the pursuit of Happiness. That to secure these rights, Governments are instituted among Men, deriving their just powers from the consent of the governed. — That whenever any Form of Government becomes destructive of these ends, it is the Right of the People to alter or to abolish it, and to institute new Government, laying its foundation on such principles and organising its powers in such form, as to them shall seem most likely to effect their Safety and Happiness.

We, therefore, the Representatives of the united States of America, in General Congress, Assembled, appealing to the Supreme Judge of the world for the rectitude of our intentions, do, in the Name, and by Authority of the good People of these Colonies, solemnly publish and declare, That these united Colonies are and of Right ought to be, **FREE AND INDEPENDENT STATES**: that they are Absolved from all Allegiance to the British Crown, and that all political connection between them and the State of Great Britain, is and ought to be totally dissolved; and that as Free and Independent States, they have full Power to levy War, conclude Peace, contract Alliances, establish Commerce, and to do all other Acts and Things which Independent States may of right do. And for the support of this Declaration, with a firm reliance on the Protection of Divine Providence, we mutually pledge to each other our Lives, our Fortunes and our sacred Honor.

The Declaration of Independence (July 4, 1776): The Spark of Sovereign Soil In Congress, July 4, 1776.

The unanimous Declaration of the thirteen united States of America... When in the course of human events, it becomes necessary for one people to dissolve the political bands which have connected them with another, and to assume among the powers of the earth the separate and equal station to which the Laws of Nature and of Nature's God entitle them, a decent respect to the opinions of mankind requires that they should declare the causes which impel them to the separation.

We hold these truths to be self-evident, that all men are created equal, that they are endowed by their Creator with certain unalienable Rights, that among these are Life, Liberty, and the pursuit of Happiness.— That to secure these rights, Governments are instituted among Men, deriving their just powers from the consent of the governed,—That whenever any Form of Government becomes destructive of these ends, it is the Right of the People to alter or to abolish it, and to institute new Government, laying its foundation on such principles and organizing its powers in such form, as to them shall seem most likely to effect their Safety and Happiness. In every stage of these Op- pressions we have Petitioned for Redress in the most humble terms: Our repeated Petitions have been answered only by repeated injury. A Prince whose character is thus marked by every act which may define a Tyrant is unfit to be the ruler of a free people.

...[The grievances list British land grabs, such as quartering troops in homes and dissolving colonial legislatures that controlled property laws.]...

And for the support of this Declaration, with a firm reliance on the protection of divine Providence, we mutually pledge to each other our Lives, our Fortunes, and our sacred Honor.

(Full text: National Archives, 2025. Property's shadow looms large— Locke's "life, liberty, property" morphed to "pursuit of happiness" to rally yeomen farmers against Crown enclosures.)

The Constitution of the United States (September 17, 1787): Wiring the Republic for Landed Liberty

We the People

of the United States, in Order to form a more perfect Union, establish Justice, insure domestic Tranquility, provide for the common defence, promote the general Welfare, and secure the Blessings of Liberty to ourselves and our Posterity, do ordain and establish this Constitution for the United States of America.

Article. I.

Section. 1.

All legislative Powers herein granted shall be vested in a Congress of the United States, which shall consist of a Senate and House of Representatives.

Section. 2.

The House of Representatives shall be composed of Members chosen every second Year by the People of the several States, and the Electors in each State shall have the Qualifications requesite for Electors of the most numerous Branch of the State Legislature.

No Person shall be a Representative who shall not have attained to the Age of twenty five Years, and been seven Years a Citizen of the United States, and who shall not, when elected, be an Inhabitant of that State in which he shall be chosen.

(The actual Enumeration shall be made within three Years after the first Meeting of the Congress of the United States, and within every subsequent Term of ten Years, in such Manner as they shall by Law direct.) The Number of Representatives shall not exceed one for every thirty Thousand, but each State shall have at Least one Representative;..

We the People of the United States, in Order to form a more perfect Union, establish Justice, insure domestic Tranquility, provide for the common defense, promote the general Welfare, and secure the Blessings of Liberty to ourselves and our Posterity, do ordain and establish this Constitution for the United States of America.

Article I (Legislative Powers – Taxing and Protecting Property):

Section 8: The Congress shall have Power To lay and collect Taxes... but all Duties, Imposts and Excises shall be uniform throughout the United States; To borrow Money on the credit of the United States; ... To regulate Commerce... To coin Money, regulate the Value thereof... To establish Post Offices and post Roads; ... To promote the Progress of Science and useful Arts... To constitute Tribunals inferior to the supreme Court; ... To make all Laws which shall be necessary and proper for carrying into Execution the foregoing Powers...

Section 9: **No Capitation, or other direct, Tax shall be laid, un less in Proportion to the Census... No Tax or Duty shall be laid on Articles exported from any State.** No Preference shall be given by any Regulation of Commerce... No Money shall be drawn from the Treasury, but in Consequence of Appropriations made by Law...

Section 10: **No State shall... pass any... Law impairing the Obligation of Contracts...**

Article IV (States' Relations):

Section 3: New States may be admitted... The Congress shall have Power to dispose of and make all needful Rules and Regulations respecting the Territory or other Property belonging to the United States...

Article VI (Supremacy Clause):

This Constitution... shall be the supreme Law of the Land...

(Takings power implied here; explicit in 5th Amendment below. Designed to prevent British-style land monopolies, ensuring states couldn't seize farms willy-nilly.)

The Bill of Rights (Ratified December 15, 1791): The Ironclad

Bill of Rights

Congress of the United States,

begun and held at the City of New-York, on Wednesday the fourth of March,
one thousand seven hundred and eighty nine.

The Conventions of a number of the States, having at the time of their adopting the Constitution, expressed
a desire, in order to present misconstruction or abuse of its powers, that further declaratory and restrictive clauses
should be added: And as extending the ground of public confidence in the Government, will best insure the
beneficent ends of its institution.—

Resolved by the Senate and House of Representatives of the United States
of America, in Congress assembled, two thirds of both Houses concurring, that the
following Articles be proposed to the Legislatures of the several States, as amendments to
the Constitution of the United States, all or any of which Articles, when ratified by three
fourths of the said Legislatures, to be valid to all intents and purposes.

Articles in addition to, and Amendment of, the Constitution of the United States of America.

proposed by Congress, and ratified by the Legislatures of the several States, pursuant to the
fifth Article of the original Constitution,

Amendment I.   Amendment II.

Congress shall make no law respecting an establishment of religion, or prohibiting the free exercise therof, or abridging
the fredom of speech, or of the press, or the right of the people peacebly to assemble, and to petition the Government
for a reders of grevences.   for a redes of grievences.

Amendment III.   Amendment IV.

A well regulated Militia, being necessary to the security of a free State, the right at conwest of the Owner, nor in time
of war, but in a manner to be prescribed by law; nor shall provate property to wakes jor jublic cus, without just
compensation.

Amendment V.   Amendment VII.

Inw nile at comnns have wher ths eliched or artbrenisery sheile excerel theonty shewn one scenunle jury of the State,
and diettent epheation the cernes eliceto hire been connuties, when neccenmus to llo the aach of rrtie tiri,
cecentlly whe cihenn of the United States.   then eccoriling to he nile of the commen tense.

Amendment VII.   Amendment VIII.

Estcaine hall shall not be cegnised, nor excesise fress negised nor crnel aud monts pronishements aflicted.

Amendment IX.   Amendment X.

The enumeration in the Constitution of curtain eghts, shall not he conscterned to thesy or disprreege ethors retisined by the people.

Amendment X.   Amendment X.

The ,recvres, and delegated to the United States by the Constitution, nor prohibuited by it to the States, cxe reserved
to the States, nespridinely or to the people.

Shield for Your Hearth and Home

Amendment I

Congress shall make no law respecting an establishment of religion, or prohibiting the free exercise thereof; or abridging the freedom of speech, or of the press; or the right of the people peaceably to assemble, and to petition the Government for a redress of grievances.

Amendment II

A well regulated Militia, being necessary to the security of a free State, the right of the people to keep and bear Arms, shall not be infringed.

Amendment III

No Soldier shall, in time of peace be quartered in any house, with out the consent of the Owner, nor in time of war, but in a manner to be prescribed by law.

Amendment IV

The right of the people to be secure in their persons, houses, pa pers, and effects, against unreasonable searches and seizures, shall not be violated, and no Warrants shall issue, but upon probable cause...

Amendment V

No person shall be held to answer for a capital... crime... nor shall any person be subject for the same offence to be twice put in jeopardy... nor shall be compelled... to be a witness against himself, **nor be deprived of life, liberty, or property, without due process of law; nor shall private property be taken for public use, without just compensation.**

Amendment VI–X [Omitted for brevity; IX protects unenumerated rights, X reserves powers to people/states—both bulwarks for local land control.]

(Full text: National Archives, 2025. The 5th's Takings Clause? Your eminent domain armor—gov can't grab your yard for a highway without paying market value.)

The Ghosts of Land Grabs: How Property Rights Have Haunted (and Hunted) Us

These documents didn't spring from a vacuum—they were battle scars from a world where kings and colonizers treated land like a poker chip. Property rights were outlined to chain the beast of arbitrary seizure: Britain's Quartering Act (1745) forced colonists to billet troops in homes, a direct assault on hearth sovereignty. The Founders, steeped in Locke's triad (life, liberty, property), saw land as the root of independence—farmers with stakes fought harder than tenants. The Constitution's Contract Clause shielded deeds from state meddling; the 5th Amendment's "just compensation" curbed crown-like eminent domain abuses.

But history's cruel irony? We wielded these rights like a club. The "first Americans" invoked the Doctrine of Discovery (upheld in 1823's Johnson v. McIntosh) to "discover" and dispossess Native nations— tribes like the Wampanoag (your notes' "People of the First Light") saw millions of acres seized via broken treaties and forced marches. By 1890, Native land holdings plummeted 98% (from 138M to 48M acres). This wasn't "progress"—it was plunder, justified as "civilizing" the frontier. Echoes? Redlining (1930s–1940s) denied Black families loans, birthing wealth gaps that persist—Black homeownership lags at 44% vs. 74% white (2025 Census).

Why study this? Because history isn't prologue—it's predator. Patterns repeat: zoning laws gatekeep suburbs like colonial enclosures; investor funds snatch starter homes, turning owners into eternal renters. Without the lens of the past, we miss how property rights built empires and empires of exclusion. Knowledge turns victims into victors—study, or be studied.

Your Call: Forge the Real Estate Revolution – Property Rights for the People, By the People

These texts birthed a nation on battle-worn soil. We can rebirth and rebuild our cities to reflect owner-occupied housing, financial freedom, and freedom of life, liberty, and the pursuit of happiness.

If you want more rights, buy property. Our Real Estate Revolution Bill of Real Estate Rights demands equal access for all: portable low-rate mortgages for everyone; zoning for the tribe, not the tycoon. Study history to create the future—build a Revolution where every family has a safe, healthy, fulfilling future, and where we live in harmony with the environment.

Revolutionary Action Steps

- **Read & Rebel**: Print these excerpts—circle property clauses, journal: "How has land power shaped *my* story?"
- **History Hunt**: Visit a Boston's Freedom Trail and Native American Sites (e.g., Wampanoag reservations)—listen to the untold Declaration.
- **Tactic Test**: In your next negotiation, channel Trump: "I'll walk— take it or share the concessions."
- **Rights Rally**: Draft your personal "Real Estate Bill of Rights"— share on X with #RealEstateRevolution.

The ink dried centuries ago, but the fight's fresh. Your home? Your fortress. Claim it.

Appendix

The Declaration of Independence:

Signed on July 4, 1776. When are you signing your Declaration of Independence from the chains that hold you back?

The average age of the signers was 45 years old. These people shaped the country going forward.

Thomas Jefferson - age 33 Principal Author

John Adams - age 40 Key Advisor, Committee of Five

Benjamin Franklin - age 70 Major Editor, Committee of Five

Rodger Sherman - age 55 Committee of Five, Key Influencer

Robert Livingston- age 29 Committee of Five

George Washington - age 44 Commander-In-Chief - Leader

John Hancock - age 39 President of Congress, first & bold signature.

Samuel Adams - age 53 Leading Radical - Ex-Tax Collector, and did NOT own a bar. His family owned a malthouse, so he did drink beer:-)

Richard Henry Lee - Age 44 Moved the resolution for independence

Thomas Paine - age 39 Did not sign The Declaration, but his writing of "Common Sense" galvanized public support for the movement towards Independence.

The Declaration of Independence: SAMPLE ONLY NOT FOR LEGAL USE:

In CONGRESS, July 4, 1776.

The unanimous Declaration of the thirteen united States of America.

When in the Course of human events, it becomes necessary for one people to dissolve the political bands which have connected them with another, and to assume among the Powers of the earth, the separate and equal station to which the Laws of Nature and of Nature's God entitle them, a decent respect to the opinions of mankind requires that they should declare the causes which impel them to the separation.

We hold these truths to be self-evident, that all men are created equal, that they are endowed by their Creator with certain unalienable Rights, that among these are Life, Liberty and the pursuit of Happiness. That to secure these rights, Governments are instituted among Men, deriving their just powers from the consent of the governed. — That whenever any Form of Government becomes destructive of these ends, it is the Right of the People to alter or to abolish it, and to institute new Government, laying its foundation on such principles and organizing its powers in such form, as to them shall seem most likely to effect their Safety and Happiness.

We, therefore, the Representatives of the united States of America, in General Congress, Assembled, appealing to the Supreme Judge of the world for the rectitude of our intentions, do, in the Name, and by Authority of the good People of these Colonies, solemnly publish and declare, That these united Colonies are and of Right ought to be, **FREE AND INDEPENDENT STATES:** that they are Absolved from all Allegiance to the British Crown, and that all political connection between them and the State of Great Britain, is and ought to be totally dissolved; and that as Free and Independent States, they have full Power to levy War, conclude Peace, contract Alliances, establish Commerce, and to do all other Acts and Things which Independent States may of right do. And for the support of this Declaration, with a firm reliance on the Protection of Divine Providence, we mutually pledge to each other our Lives, our Fortunes and our sacred Honor.

We the People

of the United States, in Order to form a more perfect Union, establish Justice, insure domestic Tranquility, provide for the common defence, promote the general Welfare, and secure the Blessings of Liberty to ourselves and our Posterity, do ordain and establish this Constitution for the United States of America.

Article. I.

Section. 1.

All legislative Powers herein granted shall be vested in a Congress of the United States, which shall consist of a Senate and House of Representatives.

Section. 2.

The House of Representatives shall be composed of Members chosen every second Year by the People of the several States, and the Electors in each State shall have the Qualifications requisite for Electors of the most numerous Branch of the State Legislature.

No Person shall be a Representative who shall not have attained to the Age of twenty five Years, and been seven Years a Citizen of the United States, and who shall not, when elected, be an Inhabitant of that State in which he shall be chosen.

(The actual Enumeration shall be made within three Years after the first Meeting of the Congress of the United States, and within every subsequent Term of ten Years, in such Manner as they shall by Law direct) The Number of Representatives shall not exceed one for every thirty Thousand, but each State shall have at Least one Representative;...

Bill Of Rights - SAMPLE ONLY NOT FOR LEGAL USE:

Bill of Rights

Congress of the United States,

begun and held at the City of New-York, on Wednesday the fourth of March,
one thousand seven hundred and eighty nine.

The Conventions of a number of the States, having at the time of their adopting the Constitution, expressed a desire, in order to present misconstruction or abuse of its powers, that further declaratory and restrictive clauses should be added: And as extending the ground of public confidence in the Government, will best insure the beneficent ends of its institution.—

Resolved by the Senate and House of Representatives of the United States of America, in Congress assembled, two thirds of both Houses concurring, that the following Articles be proposed to the Legislatures of the several States, as amendments to the Constitution of the United States, all or any of which Articles, when ratified by three fourths of the said Legislatures, to be valid to all intents and purposes.

Articles in addition to, and Amendment of, the Constitution of the United States of America.

proposed by Congress, and ratified by the Legislatures of the several States, pursuant to the fifth Article of the original Constitution.

Amendment I.   Amendment II.

Congress shall make no law respecting an establishment of religion, or prohibiting the free exercise thereof; or abridging the freedom of speech, or of the press, or the right of the people peaceably to assemble, and to petition the Government for a redress of grievances.

Amendment III.   Amendment IV.

A well regulated Militia, being necessary to the security of a free State, the right of the Owner; nor in time of war, but in a manner to be prescribed by law; nor shall private property be taken for public use, without just compensation.

Amendment V.   Amendment VII.

Amendment VII.   Amendment VIII.

Excessive bail shall not be required, nor excessive fines imposed, nor cruel and unusual punishments inflicted.

Amendment IX.   Amendment X.

The enumeration in the Constitution of certain rights, shall not be construed to deny or disparage others retained by the people.

Amendment X.   Amendment X.

The powers, and delegated to the United States by the Constitution, nor prohibited by it to the States, are reserved to the States, respectively or to the people.

Listing Agreement - SAMPLE ONLY NOT FOR LEGAL USE:

Used to outline the rules of engagement between the owner of the property and the listing agent.

This Exclusive Sale and Listing Agreement (the "Agreement") is made by and between
____ ("Seller") and ____
("Listing Broker") with regard to the real property commonly known as
____, City _____________, County ________________________________,
Massachusetts Zip _________________ ("the Property").

1. **DEFINITIONS.** (a) "MLS PIN" means MLS Property Information Network, Inc., a Massachusetts business corporation; and (b) "sell" includes a contract to sell; an exchange or contract to exchange; or an option to purchase. Listing Broker need not submit to Seller any offers to lease, rent, or enter into any agreement other than for sale of the Property.

2. **TERM.** Seller grants to Listing Broker the sole and exclusive right to list, market and sell the Property from the date of mutual acceptance of this Agreement ("Effective Date") until midnight of _____________ ("Listing Term"). If this Agreement expires while Seller is a party to a purchase and sale agreement for the Property, the Listing Term shall automatically extend until the sale is closed or the purchase and sale agreement is terminated.

3. **AGENCY.**

   a. Listing Agent. Listing Broker appoints
      to represent Seller ("Listing Agent"). This Agreement creates an agency relationship with Listing Broker and any of Listing Broker's managing brokers who supervise Listing Agent ("Supervising Broker") during the Listing Term. No other brokers affiliated with Listing Broker are agents of Seller.

   b. Pamphlet. Seller acknowledges receipt of (a) the pamphlet entitled **"Massachusetts Mandatory Licensee-Consumer Relationship Disclosure Form"**, and (b) the lead paint **"Property Transfer Notification Certification"** disclosure (if the Property was built prior to 1978), and (c) ______________________________ (add other applicable disclosure forms).

   c. Listing Broker Duties and Responsibilities. Listing Broker shall use reasonable efforts to procure a purchaser for the Property in accordance with this Agreement. Listing Broker is given authority to advertise the Property for sale, including listing the Property for sale in the MLS PIN listing service as provided in Section 9 below. Listing Broker is authorized to disclose to prospective buyers all Property information disclosed by Seller to Listing Broker, and Listing Broker shall present all offers for the Property received from prospective buyers to Seller.

   d. Listing Price. The parties agree that the initial listing price for the Property shall be $_________. The listing price may be changed by mutual agreement of the parties.

   e. Seller Cooperation. Seller agrees to cooperate with Listing Broker's reasonable efforts to market the Property and will refer all inquiries about the Property to Listing Broker.

SAMPLE ONLY NOT FOR LEGAL USE:

4. COMPENSATION. Seller has been advised and hereby acknowledges that there are no standard compensation rates for the sale of the Property, and the compensation in this Agreement is fully negotiable and not set by law. If during the Listing Term, Seller sells the Property and the sale closes, whether during or after the Listing Term; or the sale fails to close due to Seller's breach of the terms of this Agreement or the purchase and sale agreement, Seller shall pay compensation as follows:

a. <u>Listing Broker Compensation</u>.

> (a) _______% of the sales price of the Property; or
>
> (b) a flat fee of $ _____________; or
>
> (c) other amount _________________________________ (describe compensation).

Such Listing Broker compensation shall be due and payable at the closing of the sale of the Property and may be deducted from amounts held in escrow by Listing Broker in connection with the sale of the Property.

b. <u>Buyer Broker Compensation</u>.

Seller is not required to offer or provide compensation to brokers who represent a prospective buyer (a "Buyer Broker"). Before entering into this Agreement with the Seller, the Listing Broker notified the Seller that (i) MLS PIN does not require the Seller to offer compensation to Buyer Brokers or other buyer representatives (either directly or through buyers), either on or off Pinergy; and (ii) while a Buyer Broker may request compensation from the Seller in lieu of the Buyer Broker receiving any compensation from the prospective purchaser for the Buyer Broker's services on that listing, MLS PIN does not require the Seller to accede to such a request. However, Seller may authorize Listing Broker to communicate the Seller's offer of compensation to licensed Buyer Brokers (a "Buyer Broker Fee"), who procure a ready, willing and able buyer to purchase the Property. Any Buyer Broker Fee is not set by law, is fully negotiable by the parties, and shall not alter the terms of this Agreement unless the parties otherwise agree in writing. Seller hereby (*select one*):

> ☐ authorizes Listing Broker to communicate Seller's offer of a Buyer Broker Fee pursuant to the ***MLS PIN Exclusive Sale and Listing Agreement Addendum*** attached and incorporated herein.
>
> ☐ does not authorize Listing Broker to offer a Buyer Broker's Fee.

c. <u>Expiration of the Listing Term</u>. If Seller shall, within _____ days (180 days if not filled in) after the expiration of the Listing Term, sell the Property to any person to whose attention it was brought through the signs, advertising or other action of Listing Broker, or on information secured directly or indirectly from or through Listing Broker, during the Listing Term, Seller will pay Listing Broker the above compensation at closing. Provided that, if Seller pays compensation to one or more other licensed brokerage firms in conjunction with a sale of the Property, the amount of compensation payable to Listing Broker shall be reduced by the amount paid to such other listing firms.

d. <u>Cancellation Without Legal Cause</u>. If Seller cancels this Agreement without legal cause, Seller may be liable for damages incurred by Listing Broker as a result of such cancellation, regardless of whether Seller pays compensation to another licensed brokerage.

SAMPLE ONLY NOT FOR LEGAL USE:

5. **DUAL AGENCY.**

   a. <u>Listing Broker as Dual Agent</u>. Dual agency, or a dual agent relationship, where a broker represents both a seller and prospective buyer in a transaction, is allowed under Massachusetts law. However, a dual agency is only permitted if both a seller and buyer give their informed consent to such an arrangement. Having a single dual agent may facilitate a transaction, but a dual agent must act as a neutral and will not be able to favor one party's interests over the other party's. If initialed below, Seller consents to Listing Broker and Supervising Broker acting as dual agents in the sale of the Property to a buyer that Listing Broker also represents. Seller acknowledges that as a dual agent, it cannot advocate terms favorable to Seller to the detriment of the buyer.

   b. <u>Listing Broker Dual Agency</u>. If the Property is sold to a buyer represented by one of Listing Broker's agents other than Listing Agent representing the Seller ("Listing Broker's Buyer's Agent"), Seller consents to any Supervising Broker, who also supervises Listing Broker's Buyer's Agent, acting as a dual agent.

   Seller Initials: ______   Seller Initials: ___________

6. **LIST DATE.** Listing Broker shall submit the Property, including Property information and photographs of the Property (collectively the "Listing Data"), for listing and publication by MLS PIN on ________________ ("List Date"). Prior to such submission by Listing Broker, Seller shall review and confirm to Listing Broker the accuracy of the Listing Data. Seller acknowledges that exposure of the Property to the open market through MLS PIN will increase the likelihood that Seller will receive fair market value for the Property. Seller shall not materially interfere with Listing Broker's marketing of the Property. Seller may instruct   and Listing Broker must comply with Seller's request to limit marketing by not displaying the Property address or map location on the internet, by eliminating any and all internet advertising, and by imposing specific showing requirements and other similar restrictions.

7. **FAIR HOUSING.** Seller acknowledges that local, state, and federal fair housing laws prohibit discrimination based on sex, marital status, sexual orientation, gender identity, race, creed, color, religion, caste, national origin, citizenship or immigration status, families with children status, familial status, honorably discharged veteran or military status, the presence of any sensory, mental, or physical disability, or the use of a support or service animal by a person with a disability or any other status protected by federal or state law.

8. **PROPERTY ACCESS AND LOCKBOX.** Listing Broker may install a lockbox on the Property that holds a key to the Property which may be opened by participants brokers in MLS PIN, their agents, and affiliated appraiser members of MLS PIN. Unless otherwise agreed by the parties in writing, Listing Broker and other participant brokers in MLS PIN shall be entitled to show the Property at all reasonable times.

   <u>Property Access for Non-Participant Brokers</u>. Listing Broker may be contacted by licensed brokers who are not participants in MLS PIN and do not have access to the lockbox on the Property. Seller ☐ authorizes; ☐ does not authorize (authorizes if not filled in) Listing Broker to provide access to the Property to licensed brokers who are not participants in MLS PIN. If authorized, Listing Broker or other licensed agent of Listing Broker ☐ shall; ☐ shall not (shall if not filled in) be required to attend any such showing.

9. **MULTIPLE LISTING SERVICE.** Seller authorizes Listing Broker and MLS PIN to publish and distribute the Listing Data to other participants in and subscribers to MLS PIN and their affiliates and third parties for public display and other purposes, subject to any restrictions imposed by Seller. This authorization shall survive the termination of this Agreement. Listing Broker is authorized to report the sale of the Property (including price and all terms) to MLS PIN and to MLS PIN's participants and subscribers, Listing Broker may refer this listing to any other cooperating multiple listing service at Listing Broker's discretion or a licensed broker that is not a participant in or member of a multiple listing service.

Seller Disclosure: SAMPLE ONLY NOT FOR LEGAL USE:

Seller's Disclosure of known structural issues (several pages covering things like title, zoning, structural, systems, water, sewer, condo association matters, environmental matters, lead paint and other concerns. Helpful but should not be relied upon. Buyer beware!

Lead Paint Disclosure: SAMPLE ONLY NOT FOR LEGAL USE:

Used to disclose the possibility of Lead based paint, in properties build prior to 1978.

The Commonwealth of Massachusetts
Executive Office of Health and Human Services
Department of Public Health
Bureau of Environmental Health
250 Washington Street, 7th Floor
Boston, MA 02108
(800) 532-9571 / (617)-624-5757

CHILDHOOD LEAD POISONING PREVENTION PROGRAM (CLPPP)
PROPERTY TRANSFER LEAD PAINT NOTIFICATION

Under Massachusetts and federal law, this notification package must be given to prospective purchasers of homes built before 1978. This package must be given in full to meet state and federal requirements. It may be copied, as long as the type size is not made smaller. Every seller and any real estate agent involved in the sale must give this package before the signing of a purchase and sale agreement, a lease with an option to purchase, or, under state law, a memorandum of agreement used in foreclosure sales. Sellers and agents must also tell the prospective purchaser any information they know about lead in the home. They must also give a copy of any lead inspection report, risk assessment report, Letter of Compliance or Letter of Interim Control. **This package is for compliance with both state and federal lead notification requirements.**

Real estate agents must also tell prospective purchasers that under the state Lead Law, a new owner of a home built before 1978 in which a child under six will live or continue to live must have it either deleaded or brought under interim control within 90 days of taking title. This package includes a check list to certify that the prospective purchaser has been fully notified by the real estate agent. This certification should be filled out and signed by the prospective purchaser before the signing of a purchase and sale agreement, a lease with an option to purchase or a memorandum of agreement used in a foreclosure sale. It should be kept in the real estate agent's files. After getting notice, the prospective purchaser has at least 10 days, or longer if agreed to by the seller and buyer, to have a lead inspection or risk assessment if he or she chooses to have one, except in cases of foreclosure sales. There is no requirement for a lead inspection or risk assessment before a sale. A list of private lead inspectors and risk assessors licensed by the Department of Public Health is attached and can also be found on the Childhood Lead Poisoning Prevention Program's website at www.mass.gov/dph/clppp.

Sellers and real estate agents who do not meet these requirements can face a civil penalty of up to $1,000 under state law; a civil penalty of up to $10,000 and possible criminal sanctions under federal law, as well as liability for resulting damages. In addition, a real estate agent who fails to meet these requirements may be liable under the Massachusetts Consumer Protection Act.

The property transfer notification program began in 1988 and has been very successful. It provides information you need to protect your child, or your tenants' child, from lead poisoning. Massachusetts has a tax credit of up to $1,500 for each unit deleaded. There are also a number of grants and no-interest or low-interest loans available for deleading. It's up to you to do your part toward ending lead poisoning.

PLEASE TAKE THE TIME TO READ THIS DOCUMENT. LEAD POISONING IS THE NATION'S LEADING ENVIRONMENTAL HAZARD AFFECTING CHILDREN. DON'T GAMBLE WITH YOUR CHILD'S FUTURE.

CLPPP Form 94-2, 6/30/94, Rev. 2/03, Rev. 10/09

SAMPLE ONLY NOT FOR LEGAL USE:

PROPERTY TRANSFER NOTIFICATION CERTIFICATION

This form is to be signed by the prospective purchaser before signing a purchase and sale agreement or a memorandum of agreement, or by the lessee-prospective purchaser before signing a lease with an option to purchase for residential property built before 1978, for compliance with federal and Massachusetts lead-based paint disclosure requirements.

Required Federal Lead Warning Statement:
Every purchaser of any interest in residential property on which a residential dwelling was built prior to 1978 is notified that such property may present exposure to lead from lead-based paint that may place young children at risk of developing lead poisoning. Lead poisoning in young children may produce permanent neurological damage, including learning disabilities, reduced intelligence quotient, behavioral problems and impaired memory. Lead poisoning also poses a particular risk to pregnant women. The seller of any interest in residential real property is required to provide the buyer with any information on lead-based paint hazards from risk assessments or inspections in the seller's possession and notify the buyer of any known lead-based paint hazards. A risk assessment or inspection for possible lead-based paint hazards is recommended prior to purchase.

Seller's Disclosure
(a) Presence of lead-based paint and/or lead-based paint hazards (check (i) or (ii) below):
    (i)______ Known lead-based paint and/or lead-based paint hazards are present in the housing (explain).
____
    (ii)______ Seller has no knowledge of lead-based paint and/or lead-based paint hazards in the housing.
(b) Records and reports available to the seller (check (i) or (ii) below):
    (i)______ Seller has provided the purchaser with all available records and reports pertaining to lead-based paint and/or lead-based paint hazards in the housing (circle documents below).
    Lead Inspection Report; Risk Assessment Report; Letter of Interim Control; Letter of Compliance
    (ii)______ Seller has no reports or records pertaining to lead-based paint and/or lead-based paint hazards in the housing.

Purchaser's or Lessee Purchaser's Acknowledgment (initial)
(c)______ Purchaser or lessee purchaser has received copies of all documents circled above.
(d)______ Purchaser or lessee purchaser has received no documents.
(e)______ Purchaser or lessee purchaser has received the Property Transfer Lead Paint Notification.
(f)______ Purchaser or lessee purchaser has (check (i) or (ii) below):
    (i)______ received a 10-day opportunity (or mutually agreed upon period) to conduct a risk assessment or inspection for the presence of lead-based paint and/or lead-based paint hazards; or
    (ii)______ waived the opportunity to conduct a risk assessment or inspection for the presence of lead-based paint and/or lead-based paint hazards.

Agent's Acknowledgment (initial)
(g)______ Agent has informed the seller of the seller's obligations under federal and state law for lead-based paint disclosure and notification, and is aware of his/her responsibility to ensure compliance.
(h)______ Agent has verbally informed purchaser or lessee-purchaser of the possible presence of dangerous levels of lead in paint, plaster, putty or other structural materials and his or her obligation to bring a property into compliance with the Massachusetts Lead Law -- either through full deleading or interim control -- if it was built before 1978 and a child under six years old resides or will reside in the property.

Certification of Accuracy
The following parties have reviewed the information above and certify, to the best of their knowledge, that the information they have provided is true and accurate.

Seller	Date	Seller	Date
Purchaser	Date	Purchaser	Date
Agent	Date	Agent	Date

CLPPP Form 94-3, 6/30/94, Rev 9/02

Agency Disclosure Statement: SAMPLE ONLY NOT FOR LEGAL USE:

Used to disclose your agency, (who you work for and how it works). To be discussed at the first meeting of any new client.

Commonwealth of Massachusetts

BOARD OF REGISTRATION OF REAL ESTATE BROKERS AND SALESPERSONS
www.mass.gov/dpl/boards/re

MASSACHUSETTS MANDATORY REAL ESTATE LICENSEE-CONSUMER RELATIONSHIP DISCLOSURE
THIS IS NOT A CONTRACT

This disclosure is provided to you, the consumer, by the real estate licensee listed in this disclosure.

THE TIME WHEN THE REAL ESTATE LICENSEE MUST PROVIDE THIS NOTICE TO THE CONSUMER:

All real estate licensees must present this form to you at the first personal meeting with you to discuss a specific property. In the event this relationship changes, an additional disclosure must be provided and completed at that time.

CONSUMER INFORMATION AND RESPONSIBILITY:

If you are a buyer or seller, you can engage a real estate licensee to provide advice, assistance and representation to you as your agent. The real estate licensee can represent you as the seller (Seller's Agent) or represent you as the buyer (Buyer's Agent), or can assist you as a Facilitator.

All real estate licensees, regardless of the working relationship with a consumer must, by law, present properties honestly and accurately, and disclose known material defects in the real estate.

The duties of a real estate licensee do not relieve consumers of the responsibility to protect their own interests. If you need advice for legal, tax, insurance, zoning, permitted use, or land survey matters, it is your responsibility to consult a professional in those areas. Real estate licensees do not and cannot perform home, lead paint, or insect inspections, nor do they perform septic system, wetlands or environmental evaluations.

Do not assume that a real estate licensee works solely for you unless you have an agreement for that relationship.

For more detailed definitions and descriptions about real estate relationships, please see page 2 of this disclosure.

THE SELLER OR BUYER RECEIVING THIS DISCLOSURE IS HEREBY ADVISED THAT THE REAL ESTATE LICENSEE NAMED BELOW IS WORKING AS A:

Check one: ☐ Seller's agent   ☐ Buyer's agent   ☐ Facilitator

If seller's or buyer's agent is checked above, the real estate licensee must complete the following section:

Check one: ☐ Non-Designated Agency	☐ Designated Agency
The real estate firm or business listed below and all other affiliated agents are also working as the agent of the ☐ Seller ☐ Buyer	Only the licensee named herein represents the ☐ Seller ☐ Buyer (designated seller agency or designated buyer agency). In this situation any other agents affiliated with the firm or business listed below do not represent you and may represent another party in your real estate transaction.

By signing below, I, the real estate licensee, acknowledge that this disclosure has been provided to the consumer named herein:

☐ Broker ☐ Salesperson

Signature of Real Estate Licensee ___ Printed Name of Real Estate Licensee ___ License # ___ Today's Date

Name Real Estate Brokerage Firm ___ Brokerage Firm Real Estate License # ___

☐ Buyer ☐ Seller

Signature of Consumer ___ Printed Name of Consumer ___ Today's Date

☐ Buyer ☐ Seller

Signature of Consumer ___ Printed Name of Consumer ___ Today's Date

SAMPLE ONLY NOT FOR LEGAL USE:

TYPES OF AGENCY REPRESENTATION

SELLER'S AGENT

A seller can engage the services of a real estate licensee to act as the seller's agent in the sale of the seller's property. This means that the real estate agent represents the seller, who is a client. The agent owes the seller client undivided loyalty, reasonable care, disclosure, obedience to lawful instruction, confidentiality and accounting. The agent must put the seller's interests first and attempt to negotiate price and terms acceptable to their seller client. The seller may authorize sub-agents to represent him/her in marketing its property to buyers, however the seller should be aware that wrongful action by the real estate agent or sub-agents may subject the seller to legal liability for those wrongful actions.

BUYER'S AGENT

A buyer can engage the services of a real estate licensee to act as the buyer's agent in the purchase of a property. This means that the real estate agent represents the buyer, who is a client. The agent owes the buyer client undivided loyalty, reasonable care, disclosure, obedience to lawful instruction, confidentiality and accounting. The agent must put the buyer's interests first and attempt to negotiate price and terms acceptable to their buyer client. The buyer may also authorize sub-agents to represent him/her in purchasing property, however the buyer should be aware that wrongful action by the real estate agent or sub-agents may subject the buyer to legal liability for those wrongful actions.

(NON-AGENT) FACILITATOR

When a real estate licensee works as a facilitator that licensee assists the seller and/or buyer in reaching an agreement but does not represent either the seller or buyer in the transaction. The facilitator and the broker with whom the facilitator is affiliated, owe the seller and buyer a duty to present all real property honestly and accurately by disclosing known material defects and owe a duty to account for funds. Unless otherwise agreed, the facilitator has no duty to keep information received from a seller or buyer confidential. Should the seller and/or buyer expressly agree, a facilitator relationship can be changed to a seller or buyer client relationship with the written agreement of the person so represented.

DESIGNATED SELLER'S AND BUYER'S AGENT

A real estate licensee can be designated by another real estate licensee (the appointing or designating agent) to represent a buyer or seller, provided the buyer or seller expressly agrees to such designation. The real estate licensee once so designated is then the agent for that buyer or seller who becomes the agent's client. The designated agent owes the buyer client or seller client, undivided loyalty, reasonable care, disclosure, obedience to lawful instruction, confidentiality and accounting. The agent must put their client's interests first, and attempt to negotiate price and terms acceptable to their client. No other licensees affiliated with the same firm represent the client unless otherwise agreed upon by the client. In situations where the appointing agent designates another agent to represent the seller and an agent to represent the buyer in the same transaction, then the appointing agent becomes a dual agent. Consequently, a dual agent cannot fully satisfy the duties of loyalty, full disclosure, obedience to lawful instructions, which is required of a seller or buyer agent. Only your designated agent represents your interests. Written consent for designated agency must be provided before a potential transaction is identified, but in any event, no later than prior to the execution of a written agreement for purchase or sale of residential property. The consent must contain the information provided for in the regulations of the Massachusetts Board of Registration of Real Estate Brokers and Salespeople (Board). A sample consent to designated agency is available at the Board's website at www.mass.gov/dpl/re.

DUAL AGENT

A real estate licensee may act as a dual agent representing both the seller and the buyer in a transaction but only with the express and informed written consent of both the seller and the buyer. A dual agent shall be neutral with regard to any conflicting interest of the seller and buyer. Consequently, a dual agent cannot satisfy fully the duties of loyalty, full disclosure, obedience to lawful instructions, which is required of a seller or buyer agent. A dual agent does, however, still owe a duty of confidentiality of material information and accounting for funds. Written consent for dual agency must be provided before a potential transaction is identified, but in any event, no later than prior to the execution of a written agreement for purchase or sale of residential property. The consent must contain the information provided for in the regulations of the Massachusetts Board of Registration of Real Estate Brokers and Salespeople (Board). A sample consent to dual agency is available at the Board's website at www.mass.gov/dpl/re.

Buyers Agency Contract and Disclosure- SAMPLE ONLY NOT FOR LEGAL USE:

Used to bind a buyer and buyers agent.

This Buyer Broker Services Agreement ("Agreement") is effective upon mutual acceptance ("Effective Date") and is made by and between ________________("Buyer Broker") and____________________
("Buyer") for real property located in the following areas ("Area"): ________________________
(a "Property") (Area is unlimited if not filled in). Buyer appoints Buyer Broker to procure a Property of the following type: (check all that apply)

☐ Residential Single Family   ☐ Residential Multi-Family   ☐ Residential Condominium

☐ Commercial   ☐ Investment   ☐ Other____________

1. **DEFINITIONS.** "Purchase Contract" includes a contract to purchase, an offer to purchase, an exchange or contract to exchange, or an option to purchase a Property.

2. **TERM; BROKER SERVICES.** This Agreement will expire __________ days (60 days if not filled in) from the Effective Date ("Term"). If this Agreement expires while Buyer is a party to a Purchase Contract and represented by Buyer Broker as indicated on the Purchase Contract, the Term shall automatically extend until the sale is closed or the Purchase Contract is terminated.

   Buyer Broker will assist Buyer in identifying a potential Property(ies), arranging showings, reviewing financial and Property information, give general advice as to real estate acquisition rules and procedures, the structuring and negotiation of offers to purchase or other Purchase Contracts, and coordination of Buyer's efforts to identify and close on its purchase of a Property. The decision to purchase any Property rests solely with Buyer.

3. **AGENCY.**
   a. <u>Buyer Broker</u>. Buyer Broker appoints ________________________________ ("Buyer Agent") to represent Buyer. This Agreement creates an agency relationship with Buyer Broker and any of Buyer Broker's managing brokers who supervise Buyer Agent ("Supervising Broker"). No other brokers affiliated with Buyer Broker are agents of Buyer.

   b. <u>Broker Duties</u>. Buyer Broker will use reasonable efforts to locate a Property acceptable to Buyer and assist Buyer in negotiating the terms of an Offer Purchase, Purchase and Sale Agreement, or other Purchase Contract for the purchase of a Property. Buyer acknowledges that Buyer Broker and Buyer Agent may represent other potential purchasers for the same or similar properties and agrees that such representation will not constitute a breach of duty by Buyer Broker or Buyer Agent.

   c. <u>Pamphlet</u>. Buyer acknowledges receipt of (a) the pamphlet entitled **"Massachusetts Mandatory Licensee-Consumer Relationship Disclosure Form"**, and (b) the lead paint **"Property Transfer Notification Certification"** disclosure (if the Property was built prior to 1978), and (c) ________________________ (add other applicable disclosure forms).

SAMPLE ONLY NOT FOR LEGAL USE:

d. <u>Agency Relationship</u>. Buyer Broker's representation of Buyer for the purchase of a Property in the Area shall be (check one box):

☐ <u>Exclusive</u>. Buyer may not enter into an agency relationship with another real estate firm during the Term for the purchase of a Property in the Area ("Exclusive Agency"); or

☐ <u>Non-Exclusive</u>. Buyer may enter into a non-exclusive agency relationship with other real estate firms during the Term ("Non-Exclusive Agency").

4. DUAL AGENCY.

<u>Buyer Broker as Dual Agent</u>. Dual agency, or a dual agent relationship, where a broker represents both a seller and prospective buyer in a transaction, is allowed under Massachusetts law. However, a dual agency is only permitted if both a seller and buyer give their informed consent to such an arrangement. A dual agent may facilitate a transaction, but a dual agent must remain neutral and is prohibited from favoring one party's interests over the other party's. If initialed below, Buyer consents to Buyer Broker, Supervising Broker and/or Buyer Agent acting as dual agents in the sale of a Property to Buyer where Buyer Broker, Supervising Broker and/or Buyer Agent also represent the seller. Buyer acknowledges that, as a dual agent, Buyer Broker, Supervising Broker and/or Buyer Agent cannot advocate terms favorable to Buyer to the detriment of a seller. If initialed below, Buyer consents to Buyer Broker, Supervising Broker and/or Buyer Agent acting as limited dual agents in the sale of property that is listed by Buyer Broker.

Buyer's Initials Date	Buyer's Initials Date

5. **COMPENSATION.** Buyer acknowledges that there are no standard compensation rates and the compensation in this Agreement is fully negotiable and not set by law. Buyer Broker may not receive any compensation for brokerage services provided to Buyer from any source greater than the amounts set forth in this Section 5 or any subsequent amendment hereto. If during the Term, Buyer enters into an agreement to purchase a Property, and (i) the sale closes, whether during or after the Listing Term, or (ii) the sale fails to close due to Buyer's breach of the terms of this Agreement, or the Purchase Contract, Buyer Broker shall be entitled to compensation (the "Compensation") as follows:

a. <u>Standard Compensation</u>.

(a) _______% of the sales price of the Property; or

(b) a flat fee of $ ____________; or

(c) other amount _________________________ (describe compensation).

b. If Buyer Broker is a dual agent pursuant to Section 4 above, and represents both Buyer and the seller, then the Compensation shall be (equal to the amount in subsection 5(a) if not filled in).

(a) _______% of the sales price of the Property; or

(b) a flat fee of $ ___________; or

(c) other amount _________________________ (describe compensation).

Offer to Purchase: SAMPLE ONLY NOT FOR LEGAL USE:

Initial Document used to secure the property. Looking for basic agreement on price, timing, and conditions. Followed usually by an inspection and then Purchase in Sale.

Date: ________________

From: ______________________________ ("Buyer")   TO: ______________________________ ("Seller")

______________________________   ______________________________

______________________________   ______________________________

Massachusetts licensed real estate broker/salesperson ______________________ presents this Offer to Purchase ("Offer") and is acting in this transaction, pursuant to a separate agreement as (check one):

    □ BUYER's Agent   □ SELLER's Agent   □ Facilitator   □ Dual Agent

The property subject to this Offer is identified as follows: ______________________________
(*Property Address*), and includes all improvements, fixtures, and equipment located thereon (the "Property").

Special provisions (if any) re fixtures, appliances, etc.:

____

Buyer offers to buy the Property under the following terms and conditions:

1. **Purchase Price**. Buyer will pay the sum of $____________ for the Property, of which:

    a. ______________________ is paid as a deposit to bind this Offer

    b. ______________________ to be paid as an additional deposit upon the execution of the Purchase and Sale Agreement provided for below.

    c. ______________________ is to be paid at the time of delivery of the Deed by certified or bank check(s) or wire transfer of immediately available funds.

    d. ______________________ Total Purchase Price.

2. **Duration of Offer**. This Offer is valid until __________ (*Time*) on __________ (*Date*), at or before which time a copy hereof shall be signed by Seller, signifying acceptance of this Offer, and returned to Buyer, otherwise this Offer shall be considered rejected and any deposit shall be promptly returned to Buyer.

3. **Purchase and Sale**. Buyer and Seller shall, on or before __________ (*Date*), execute a Purchase and Sale Agreement, or other agreement mutually acceptable to the parties, which, when executed, shall be the agreement between the parties.

4. **Closing**. A Deed, conveying good and clear record, marketable and insurable title, shall be delivered by Seller to Buyer at __________ (*Time*), on __________ (*Closing Date*) at a mutually agreeable location.

5. **Deposit**. The deposit shall be held by ______________________, as escrow agent, subject to the terms of this Offer. If Buyer does not fulfill its obligations under this Offer, the deposit shall forthwith be paid to Seller, without recourse to either party. In the event of any disagreement between the parties, the escrow agent may retain the deposit pending instructions mutually given by the parties. A similar provision shall be included in the Purchase and Sale Agreement with respect to any deposits held under its terms. The escrow agent shall abide by any Court decision as to whom the funds shall be paid and shall not be made a party to any lawsuit as a result of acting as escrow agent. If the escrow agent is made a party in violation of this paragraph, Seller and Buyer shall immediately take all action necessary to have the escrow agent dismissed from the lawsuit and the party asserting a claim against the escrow agent shall pay the escrow agent's reasonable attorneys' fees and costs.

SAMPLE ONLY NOT FOR LEGAL USE:

6. **Compensation to Buyer Broker.** (*Delete if N/A*) The Buyer's obligations under this agreement are subject to Seller's agreement to pay ________ % of the sale price of the Property, or a flat fee of $________ to _______________________ ("Buyer Broker") at the time of closing.

7. **Contingencies.** The initialed Riders, if any, attached hereto are incorporated herein by reference.

___**Mortgage Contingency (check if applicable):** Buyer's obligation to purchase the Property is subject to Buyer obtaining a written commitment for mortgage financing from a conventional bank or other institutional lender in the amount of $________ at prevailing rates, terms and conditions, by ________. If, despite reasonable efforts, Buyer is unable to obtain such commitment, Buyer may terminate this Offer by written notice to Seller or Seller's broker, by 5:00 p.m. on the day set forth above. Upon receipt of such notice, this Offer shall terminate without recourse to the parties, and any deposit made by Buyer shall be returned. The failure of Buyer to provide timely notice of termination to Seller shall constitute a waiver of Buyer's right to terminate this Offer on account of this contingency.

Home Inspection Contingency (check one box as applicable):

___ This Offer is subject to Buyer obtaining a home inspection on the Property, including, but not limited to, home structure and systems, pest, radon and lead paint, on or before ________, from a person of Buyer's choosing. If the inspection is not acceptable to Buyer in Buyer's sole discretion, Buyer may terminate this Offer by written notice to Seller or Seller's broker, by 5:00 p.m. on the day set forth above. Upon receipt of such notice, this Offer shall terminate without recourse to the parties, and any deposit made by Buyer shall be returned. The failure of Buyer to provide timely notice of termination to Seller shall constitute a waiver of the Buyer's right to terminate this Offer on account this Offer on account of this contingency.

___ This Offer is not subject to Buyer obtaining a home inspection on the Property because the proposed sale is exempt under the provisions of 760 Code of Massachusetts Regulations 74.00.

___ **Other** (if checked, complete and attach applicable Rider)

8. **Additional terms.** Additional terms and conditions, if any:

____

9. **Time is of the essence as to each provision of this Offer.**

Buyer Acknowledgments. Buyer acknowledges (i) receipt of a Massachusetts Mandatory Real Estate Licensee-Consumer Agency Disclosure, Property Transfer Lead Paint Notification and Certification (for residences built before 1978) and Home Inspectors Facts for Consumers brochure (prepared by the Massachusetts Office of Consumer Affairs), and (ii) Massachusetts Mandatory Residential Home Inspection Disclosure. Buyer has not relied upon any representation, oral or written, from Seller or any real estate broker concerning the legal use of, or the condition of, the Property. Buyer acknowledges that in making this Offer there are no warranties or representations made by Seller or any broker on which Buyer has relied, except as set forth in this Offer.

Buyer/Seller Acknowledgements. Buyer and Seller acknowledge receipt of a signed Massachusetts Mandatory Residential Home Inspection Disclosure.

Purchase and Sale Contract: SAMPLE ONLY NOT FOR LEGAL USE:

These are usually drafted by your attorney and can run 10-20 pages of legal verbiage. Used to firmly bind the transaction and collect deposit money to be held in escrow by listing Broker until closing. This is a critical step. Once you've reach this point, it's usually time to start packing your bags.

This Purchase and Sale Agreement (this "Agreement") entered into by the Parties as of _____________________, 20___, sets forth the terms pursuant to which the Seller identified below agrees to sell, and the Buyer identified below agrees to buy, the Premises described in this Agreement.

Section 1.   BASIC INFORMATION

Seller (Name(s) and Address):	Buyer (Name(s) and Address):
Seller's Notice Address and Email:	Buyer's Notice Address and Email:
Seller's Attorney (Name/Address/Tel/Email):	Buyer's Attorney (Name/Address/Tel/Email):

Parties: Seller and Buyer

Premises: The land, together with the buildings, structures, and other improvements located on the land, known as and numbered ____________________________________, Massachusetts. For title reference purposes only, see Deed recorded with the ______________________ Registry of Deeds/Registry District of the Land Court (the "Registry of Deeds") in Book __________, Page ______/as Document No. ________________.

   Included Items. The following items are included in the sale of the Premises, at no additional cost, in addition to those items listed in Section 2 of this Agreement:

      [ ] solar panels: _____ leased _____ owned
      [ ] other: list ______

   Excluded Items. The following items are excluded from the sale and will be removed from the Premises by Seller prior to the Closing:

      [Indicate any leased equipment that will need to be removed unless the lease can be assigned: ___________]

Closing Disclosure - SAMPLE ONLY NOT FOR LEGAL USE:

Outlines all the costs associated with the real estate transfer and financing at closing. Filled out by an attorney and closing/title company.

Closing Disclosure

OMB Control No. 1024-0045

This form is a statement of final loan terms and closing costs. Compare this document with your Loan Estimate.

Closing Information

Date Issued: 01/31/2026
Closing Date: 02/15/2026
Disbursement Date: 02/15/2026
Settlement Agent: Hometown Title Company
File #: 123456789

Property: 123 Main Street, Boston, MA 02101

Transaction Information

Borrower: John Q. Public & Jane M. Public
Seller: Michael Seller & Sarah Seller
Lender: First National Mortgage Company

Sale Price: $500,000.00

Loan Terms

Can this amount increase after closing?

Loan Amount: $400,000.00	NO
Interest Rate: 6.125%	NO
Monthly Principal & Interest: $2,429.48	NO

Prepayment Penalty: NO
Balloon Payment: NO

Projected Payments

Payment Calculation	Years 1-30
Principal & Interest	$2,429.48
Mortgage Insurance	—
Estimated Escrow	$625.00
Property Taxes	$375.00
Homeowner's Insurance	$150.00
Other: HOA Dues	$100.00
Estimated Total Monthly Payment	$3,054.48

Costs at Closing

Closing Costs	
Total Closing Costs (J)	$18,475.00
Closing Costs Paid Before Closing	-$500.00
Closing Costs Financed	$0.00

Cash to Close	
Down Payment/Funds from Borrower	$100,000.00
Deposit	-$25,000.00
Funds for Borrower	$0.00
Seller Credits	-$5,000.00
Adjustments and Other Credits	-$250.00
Cash to Close	$88,225.00

SAMPLE ONLY NOT FOR LEGAL USE:

Closing Cost Details

Loan Costs

Description	Borrower-Paid At Closing	Seller-Paid At Closing
A. Origination Charges		
Loan Origination Fee (1%)	$4,000.00	—
Discount Points (0.5%)	$2,000.00	—
Application Fee	—	—
Underwriting Fee	$500.00	—
Total Origination Charges	**$6,500.00**	**—**
B. Services Borrower Did Not Shop For		
Appraisal Fee	$750.00	—
Credit Report Fee	$50.00	—
Flood Determination Fee	$20.00	—
Tax Service Fee	$85.00	
Total Services Borrower Did Not Shop For	**$905.00**	**—**
C. Services Borrower Did Shop For		
Title - Lender's Title Insurance	$1,200.00	—
Title - Settlement/Closing Fee	$500.00	$500.00
Title - Title Search	$300.00	—
Survey Fee	$450.00	—
Attorney Fee	$1,500.00	$1,500.00
Home Inspection Fee (paid before closing)	—	—
Total Services Borrower Did Shop For	**$3,950.00**	**$2,000.00**
D. TOTAL LOAN COSTS (A + B + C)	**$11,355.00**	**$2,000.00**

Other Costs

Description	Borrower-Paid At Closing	Seller-Paid At Closing
E. Taxes and Other Government Fees		
Recording Fees - Deed: $125.00 Mortgage: $125.00	$125.00	$125.00
Transfer Tax - State: $2,000 County: $500	—	$2,500.00
Total Taxes and Government Fees	**$125.00**	**$2,625.00**
F. Prepaids		

SAMPLE ONLY NOT FOR LEGAL USE:

Closing Disclosure - SAMPLE

Description	Borrower-Paid At Closing	Seller-Paid At Closing
Homeowner's Insurance Premium (12 months)	$1,800.00	–
Mortgage Insurance Premium (___months)	–	–
Prepaid Interest ($67.36 per day from 2/15/26 to 3/1/26)	$1,010.40	–
Property Taxes (___months)	–	–
Total Prepaids	$2,810.40	–
G. Initial Escrow Payment at Closing		
Homeowner's Insurance per month for 2 months	$300.00	–
Mortgage Insurance per month for ___months	–	–
Property Taxes per month for 4 months	$1,500.00	–
Aggregate Adjustment	–$384.60	–
Total Initial Escrow Payment	$1,415.40	–
H. Other		
Owner's Title Insurance (optional)	$1,500.00	–
HOA Transfer Fee	$250.00	–
Home Warranty	$500.00	–
Real Estate Commission (Buyer's Agent 2.5%)	–	$12,500.00
Real Estate Commission (Seller's Agent 2.5%)	–	$12,500.00
Total Other	$2,250.00	$25,000.00
I. TOTAL OTHER COSTS (E + F + G + H)	$6,600.60	$27,625.00
J. TOTAL CLOSING COSTS (D + I)	$17,955.60	$29,625.00

Declaration Of Real Estate Independence

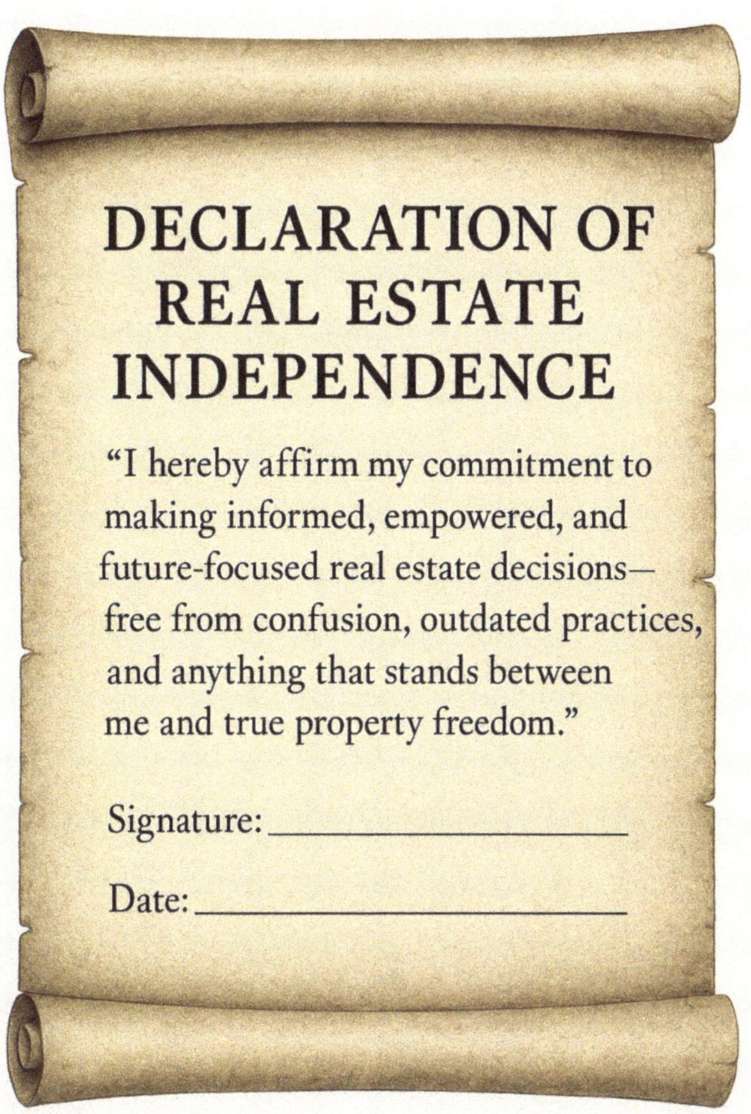

Get used to signing important documents. It's part of making a commitment.

Your signature is your bond.

Glossary

Housing and Mortgage Terms:

Acceleration Clause

A provision in a mortgage allowing the lender to demand full repayment if payments are missed or default occurs.

Adjustable Rate Mortgage (ARM)

A mortgage with an interest rate that changes periodically based on market conditions and an index.

Amortization

The process of gradually paying off a debt through scheduled payments over time, covering principal and interest.

Annual Percentage Rate (APR)

The total yearly cost of a mortgage as a percentage, including interest, fees, and other charges.

Appraisal

An expert estimate of a property's value, required by lenders to confirm the loan amount.

Appreciation

The increase in a property's market value over time due to market conditions or improvements.

Asbestos

A toxic material once used in insulation; banned in new homes but may exist in older properties, posing health risks.

Assets

Everything of value owned by an individual, such as savings, investments, or property.

Assumption

A buyer's agreement to take over the seller's existing mortgage, assuming responsibility for payments.

Automated Clearing House (ACH)

An electronic network for automatic monthly withdrawals from a bank account for mortgage payments.

Balloon Loan

A mortgage with low payments for a short term, followed by a large lump-sum payment at the end.

Basis Point

1/100th of a percentage point (0.01%), used to express changes in interest rates.

Biweekly Mortgage

A payment plan with half the monthly amount paid every two weeks, resulting in 26 payments yearly for faster payoff.

Break-Even Point

The time it takes for interest savings from buying points or refinancing to equal the upfront costs.

Bridge Loan

A short-term loan to finance a new home purchase before selling the current one.

Building Code

Local regulations ensuring homes meet safety and construction standards; certification confirms compliance.

Capacity

A borrower's ability to make mortgage payments based on income, debts, and obligations.

Caps

Limits on how much an ARM's interest rate or payments can increase in a period or over the loan's life.

Cash-Out Refinance

Refinancing a mortgage for more than owed, taking the difference in cash for other uses.

Certificate of Eligibility

A VA document confirming a veteran's eligibility for a VA loan guarantee.

Certificate of Occupancy

Official approval that a home is safe and ready for habitation after construction or renovations.

Closing

The final step in a mortgage where ownership transfers, documents are signed, and funds are exchanged.

Closing Costs

Fees paid at closing, including origination, appraisal, title insurance, and taxes.

Co-Borrower

A person jointly obligated on a mortgage, sharing ownership and repayment responsibility.

Co-Signer

Someone who signs a loan to guarantee repayment but does not own the property.

Collateral

Property pledged as security for a loan, such as a home for a mortgage.

Comparables (Comps)

Recently sold similar properties used to determine a home's market value.

Conforming Loan

A mortgage meeting Fannie Mae and Freddie Mac guidelines for purchase on the secondary market.

Construction Loan

A short-term loan funding home building, disbursed in stages as work progresses.

Contingency

A contract clause allowing a buyer to back out if conditions (e.g., inspection) aren't met.

Conventional Loan

A mortgage not insured or guaranteed by the government, typically requiring good credit and down payment.

Credit Report

A document detailing a borrower's credit history, scores, and debts used in loan approval.

Credit Score

A numerical rating (e.g., FICO) of creditworthiness, influencing loan terms and rates.

Curb Appeal

The visual attractiveness of a home's exterior to potential buyers from the street.

Debt-to-Income Ratio (DTI)

The percentage of gross monthly income used for debt payments, including mortgage.

Deed

A legal document transferring property ownership from seller to buyer.

Default

Failure to meet mortgage terms, such as missing payments, leading to potential foreclosure.

Discount Points

Upfront fees paid to lower the interest rate; one point equals 1% of the loan amount.

Down Payment

The initial cash payment toward a home's purchase price, typically 3–20%.

Earnest Money

A deposit made by a buyer showing good faith, applied to closing costs if the deal closes.

Easement

The right to use part of another's property, like a shared driveway.

Encroachment

Unauthorized use of neighboring property, such as a fence crossing boundaries.

Equity

The home's market value minus the remaining mortgage balance.

Escrow

Funds held by a neutral third party for taxes and insurance, or documents until closing.

Escrow Account

An account managed by the lender for paying property taxes and insurance from monthly payments.

Fannie Mae

Federal National Mortgage Association; buys conforming loans to provide liquidity to lenders.

Federal Housing Administration (FHA)

Government agency insuring loans for borrowers with lower credit or down payments.

Fixed-Rate Mortgage

A loan with an unchanging interest rate and payments for the entire term.

Fixed-Term Deposit

A savings account with a set term and rate, often used for down payment funds.

Flip

Buying a property at a low price, renovating, and reselling for profit.

Foreclosure

Legal process where a lender seizes and sells a home due to unpaid mortgage.

Freddie Mac

Federal Home Loan Mortgage Corporation; similar to Fannie Mae, supports mortgage market liquidity.

Ginnie Mae

Government National Mortgage Association; guarantees timely payments on government-backed loans.

Good Faith Estimate (GFE)

An early disclosure of estimated closing costs and loan terms from the lender.

Government-Sponsored Enterprise (GSE)

Entities like Fannie Mae and Freddie Mac that buy and securitize mortgages.

Hazard Insurance

Coverage for damage to a home from events like fire, wind, or theft.

Home Equity Line of Credit (HELOC)

A revolving credit line secured by home equity, with variable rates.

Home Equity Loan

A lump-sum loan secured by home equity, often with fixed rates.

Home Inspection

A professional examination of a property's condition before purchase.

Homeowner's Association (HOA)

An organization managing shared spaces in a community, collecting fees for maintenance.

Housing Expense Ratio

Percentage of income allocated to housing costs like mortgage, taxes, and insurance.

HUD

U.S. Department of Housing and Urban Development; oversees housing programs and FHA.

Index

A benchmark rate (e.g., LIBOR) used to adjust ARM interest rates.

Interest Rate

The percentage of the loan principal charged annually for borrowing money.

Jumbo Loan

A mortgage exceeding conforming loan limits set by Fannie Mae and Freddie Mac.

Lender Credit

A credit from the lender toward closing costs in exchange for a higher interest rate.

Lien

A legal claim on a property as security for a debt, like a mortgage.

Loan Estimate

A form detailing the loan terms, monthly payments, and closing costs provided early in the process.

Loan Officer

A professional who helps borrowers apply for and secure a mortgage.

Loan Origination Fee

A fee charged by the lender for processing and funding the loan, often 1% of the amount.

Loan-to-Value Ratio (LTV)

The loan amount divided by the property's appraised value, expressed as a percentage.

Lock-In

A lender's commitment to hold a specific interest rate for a set period.

Maintenance

Ongoing costs to keep a property in good condition, like repairs and upkeep.

Margin

A fixed percentage added to an ARM's index to determine the interest

rate.

Market Value

The current estimated price a property would sell for in the open market.

Mortgage

A loan secured by real property, using the home as collateral for repayment.

Mortgage Broker

An intermediary who shops multiple lenders for the best mortgage terms.

Mortgage Insurance Premium (MIP)

Insurance required for FHA loans to protect the lender against default.

Multiple Listing Service (MLS)

A database of properties for sale, used by real estate agents.

No-Closing-Cost Mortgage

A loan where the lender covers closing costs, often by increasing the interest rate.

Non-Conforming Loan

A mortgage that doesn't meet Fannie Mae/Freddie Mac standards, like jumbo loans.

Origination Points

Fees for creating the loan, separate from discount points.

Owner Financing

Seller provides the mortgage directly to the buyer, bypassing traditional lenders.

PITI

Acronym for principal, interest, taxes, and insurance in a monthly mortgage payment.

Planned Unit Development (PUD)

A community with mixed land uses like housing and recreation, governed by rules.

Pre-Approval

A lender's conditional commitment for a loan amount based on credit review.

Prepaid Interest

Interest paid at closing for the period from closing to the first payment.

Prepayment Penalty

A fee for paying off a loan early, common in some ARMs or subprime loans.

Principal

The original loan amount borrowed, excluding interest.

Private Mortgage Insurance (PMI)

Insurance protecting the lender if the borrower defaults, required for conventional loans under 20% down.

Property Tax

Local government taxes based on a home's assessed value, paid annually or escrowed.

Rate Lock

Agreement to secure an interest rate for a specified time during processing.

Real Estate Agent

Licensed professional representing buyers or sellers in property transactions.

Refinance

Replacing an existing mortgage with a new one, often for better terms or cash.

Rent-to-Own

An agreement where rent payments build toward a future home purchase.

Reverse Mortgage

A loan for homeowners 62+ allowing them to convert home equity into cash without monthly payments.

Revolution Bond

Proposed fund for home buyers locked at 3% for life.

Secondary Mortgage Market

System where loans are sold to investors after origination, freeing lender capital.

Subprime Loan

A higher-risk mortgage for borrowers with poor credit, often with higher rates.

Sustainable City

A city designed with consideration for social, economic, and environmental impacts, while providing a resilient, inclusive habitat that meets current residents' needs without compromising future generations' ability to do the same.

Survey

A detailed map showing property boundaries, structures, and improvements.

Title Insurance

Protection against losses from defects in property ownership, like liens or fraud.